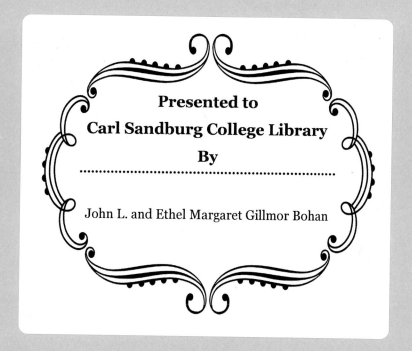

Structure and Surface

Contemporary Japanese Textiles

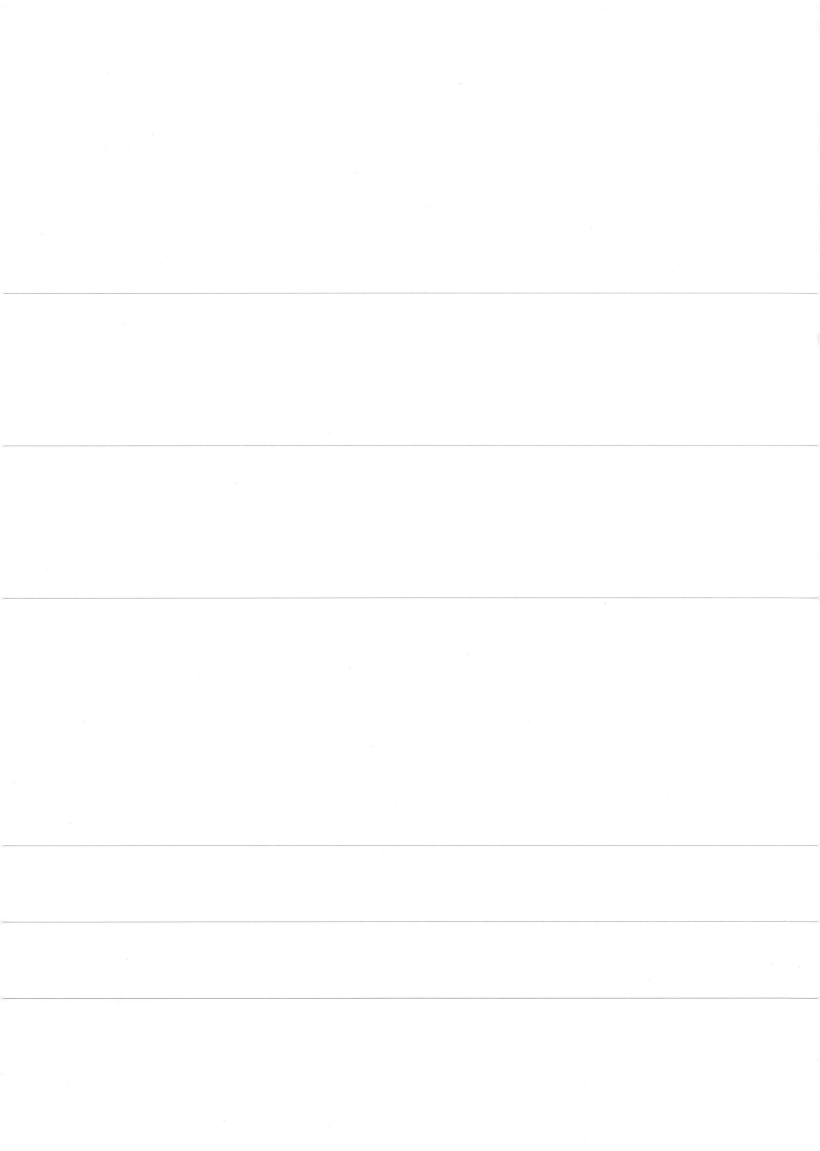

Structure and Surface

Contemporary Japanese Textiles

Cara McCarty and Matilda McQuaid

The Museum of Modern Art, New York

Distributed by Harry N. Abrams, Inc., New York

Published on the occasion of the exhibition
*Structure and Surface: Contemporary Japanese
Textiles*, organized by Matilda McQuaid,
Associate Curator in the Department of
Architecture and Design, The Museum of
Modern Art, New York, and Cara McCarty,
Curator of Decorative Arts and Design,
The Saint Louis Art Museum, November 12,
1998 to January 26, 1999.

The exhibition will travel to The Saint Louis
Art Museum, June 18 to August 15, 1999.

The exhibition is made possible by the AT&T
Foundation and by the Contemporary
Exhibition Fund of The Museum of Modern
Art, established with funds from Lily
Auchincloss, Agnes Gund and Daniel Shapiro,
and Jo Carole and Ronald S. Lauder.

Additional generous support is provided by
Toray Industries, Inc., Dorothy and Lewis B.
Cullman, Toyota Motor Sales, U.S.A., Inc.,
the Pola Art Foundation, Asahi Glass Co.,
Ltd., and Urase Company, Ltd.

This publication is made possible by the
Japan Foundation.

Special thanks to Karin Willis for her
photography of the textiles.

Produced by the Department of Publications,
The Museum of Modern Art, New York
Edited by Jasmine Moorhead
Designed by Patrick Seymour, Ji Lee —
Tsang Seymour Design, New York
Production by Christopher Zichello
Printed by Toppan Printing Company, Ltd.,
Tokyo

Library of Congress Catalogue Card Number
98-067047. ISBN 0-87070-076-6 (The
Museum of Modern Art). ISBN 0-8109-
6190-3 (Harry N. Abrams, Inc.)

Published by The Museum of Modern Art,
11 West 53 Street, New York, New York
10019. (www.moma.org)

Distributed in the United States and Canada
by Harry N. Abrams, Inc., New York
Distributed outside the United States and
Canada by Thames and Hudson, Ltd., London

Printed in Japan

Cover: Urase Company, Ltd. *Harmony*. 1997.
Polyester. Heat-transfer printed

Photograph Credits

Contents

Preface

Newspaper, banana fiber, copper, stainless steel, and feathers are woven among silk, cotton, wool, linen, and polyester in today's Japanese textiles. These often unlikely juxtapositions of materials assembled using an array of construction techniques have resulted in works of astonishing beauty and creativity that reassert the artistic potential of textiles. Most of the pieces selected for this catalogue and exhibition were made in the last five years and represent some of the finest and most imaginative textiles by artists, designers, and manufacturers currently working with fiber, cloth, and fashion.

For centuries Japan has been associated with a rich textile tradition and was a leading center of cotton and silk production, but in recent years it has reemerged as an influential and vital force in this industry. The innovative fabrication processes employed in the works presented here are the culmination of four decades of textile research, development, and invention which has matured into a full-fledged movement with an international impact. The ingenious convergence of mechanical and industrial techniques with labor-intensive hand-work poignantly captivates and symbolizes our contemporary spirit.

Since the 1980s we have each made several trips to Japan to study the vast and flourishing activity, visiting textile producing centers in Kiryu, Fukui, and the Kyoto region, handweavers in Okinawa, and many small but technically sophisti-cated factories. We continue to be enraptured by what we have seen, and this exhibition, jointly organized by The Museum of Modern Art and The Saint Louis Art Museum, is a celebration of these textile treasures. Normally an installation of this range would draw from several cultures, but all the works come from one country not quite as large as California. Even so, the textiles repre-sent only some of the many artists and designers whose accomplishments are too numerous to display in one exhibition. By documenting these magical and masterful artworks, we hope to sensitize our culture to the continually expanding boundaries and possibilities for creating textiles.

Cara McCarty
Curator
Decorative Arts and Design
THE SAINT LOUIS ART MUSEUM

Matilda McQuaid
Associate Curator
Department of Architecture and Design
THE MUSEUM OF MODERN ART, NEW YORK

Opposite: Detail of pleated fabric from
Inoue Pleats Company

Acknowledgments

This publication is dedicated to Sheila Hicks. Throughout the project she provided constant encouragement and support and was exceedingly generous in sharing information, her time, and her vast knowledge about textiles. She made known all her sources in Japan, opening many doors for us and then letting us pick and choose from our perspective as museum curators. Her editorial comments greatly enhanced both of our essays and helped refine our thoughts.

Numerous individuals have been extremely helpful throughout our travels and research in Japan. We regret there is not sufficient room to acknowledge them in detail but have tremendous gratitude for them all—this exhibition and publication are a tribute to each and every one. In particular we would like to thank the artists, designers, and manufacturers who opened up their studios, workshops, and factories and shared their world with us. Many of them graciously revealed secrets of their art, disclosing their well-guarded processes that here are documented publicly for the first time.

Filmmaker Cristobal Zañartu and producer Rebecca Clark deserve special recognition. When we met they were producing a series of films that document the textile culture in Japan today, and we were particularly intrigued with their footage of the artists working in remote regions of Japan. We had already been gathering information about textile designers in the Tokyo area, so we joined their pioneering efforts and investigated further.

Reiko Sudo of Nuno Corporation and Junichi Arai were two of the first designers we met, and throughout the entire project they have been extremely cooperative and enthusiastic. Issey Miyake and Makiko Minagawa of Miyake Design Studio, with Jun Kanai and Nancy Knox of Issey Miyake USA Corporation have been incredibly forthcoming with assistance. Koichi Yoshimura of S. Yoshimura Co., Ltd., made certain that we saw the most innovative factories in the Fukui prefecture. Individual artists we would like to acknowledge are Akiko Ishigaki, Masakazu Kobayashi, Naomi Kobayashi, Chiaki Maki, Kaori Maki, Yuh Okano, Hiroyuki Shindo, Toshiko Taira, Hideko Takahashi, Chiyoko Tanaka, Jun Tomita, and Michiko Uehara. Many of them have created works specifically for this exhibition.

The textile designers and manufacturers we especially wish to thank are Kunio Satake and Masami Kikuchi of Bridgestone Metalpha Corporation; Mikio Inayama, Yuuichi Inayama, and Yoshiyuki Matsuda of Inayama Textile Inc.; Katsuhiro Inoue, Hiroshi Sako, Chikayoshi Shirasaki, and Yaichiro Nakamura of Inoue Pleats Co., Ltd.; Sokichi Kaneko and Akihiro Kaneko of Kaneko Orimono Co., Ltd.; Yoshiyasu Arai of Kay Tay Textile Inc.; Yoshihiro Kimura of Kimura Senko Co., Ltd.; Jürgen Lehl and Eva Takamine of Jürgen Lehl Co., Ltd.; Akihiro Mita and Osamu Mita of Mitasho Co., Ltd.; Eiji Miyamoto of Miyashin Co., Ltd.; at Nuno Corporation, Keiji Otani, Hiroko Suwa, and Sayuri Shimoda, along with Yoko Obi, Yuka Taniguchi, Mari Ohno, Kazuhiro Ueno, Kazue Tamagawa, Ryoko Sugiura, Mizue Okada, Yukiko Takahashi; Ryoji Sakai of Sakase Adtech Co., Ltd.; Yoshiharu Sakai of Sakase Textile Co., Ltd.; Shinichiro Ohkubo at Teijin Limited; Takanobu Shibuya, Kenji Yamazaki, and Ikuhisa Ishikawa of Toray Industries Inc.; Chisato Tsumori; Nobutaka Urase and Shigemi Matsuyama of Urase Co., Ltd.; and Masaji Yamazaki and Hiroki Yamazaki of Yamazaki Vellodo Co., Ltd.

This exhibition would not have been possible without funding from the AT&T Foundation and the Contemporary Exhibition Fund of The Museum of Modern Art. We are also grateful to Dorothy and Lewis B. Cullman; Toray Industries, Inc.; Toyota Motor Sales, U.S.A., Inc.; and the Pola Art Foundation. The publication is made possible by the Japan Foundation, and Urase Co., Ltd., donated the fabric for its extraordinary cover. Asahi Glass Co., Ltd., provided the magnificent lighting of the exhibition.

Other people who deserve recognition are Takeo Ohbayashi of Obayashi Corp.; Kenjiro Shinohara and Masaru Igarashi of Itochu Gallery Co., Ltd., for their tireless fund-raising efforts; Shozo Toyohisa of Kilt Planning Office, Inc., for his extraordinary lighting design; Craig Konyk for reading the manuscript; Yasuki Hashimoto and Akane Nakabayashi at Opra; S.G.F. Associates Inc.; Kayoko Ota for her translating talents; Emily Rauh Pulitzer; Katharina Belting at the Japan Society; Yaffa Gaon; Seiju Toda; Kazuko Koike, Director of Sagacho Exhibit Space in Tokyo; Richard Martin at The Metropolitan Museum of Art's Costume Institute; Mieko Taira; Betty Hoffman; Amanda Mayer Stinchecum; Yoshiki Hishinuma; Takahisa Suzuki; The Textile Research Center, Kiryu; and Akira Mishima. The elegant installation design by architect Toshiko Mori, with Sheila Choi, enhanced the beauty of the works.

Special thanks go to research assistants Mari Nakahara and Yoshiko Yoneyama whose invaluable help with translations, correspondence, cataloguing, and compiling documentation was indispensable and facilitated the project at all steps of the way.

Many colleagues at both institutions helped make the exhibition possible. At The Museum of Modern Art we are especially grateful to Glenn D. Lowry, Director, and Terence Riley, Chief Curator of the Department of Architecture and Design, for their early enthusiasm; Jennifer Russell, Deputy Director for Exhibitions and Collections Support, for her ongoing encouragement; in the Department of the Deputy Director for Development, Michael Margitich, Monika Dillon, and Kyle Miscia; Jennifer Herman in the Department of Development and Membership; Jay Levenson, Director of the International Program; Eleni Cocordas for her mountain of encouragement and belief in the exhibition; Lynda Zycherman and Roger Griffith in Conservation; Patterson Sims, Deputy Director for Education and Research Support; Josiana Bianchi and Janet Stewart in the Department of Education; Diane Farynyk, Linda Karsteter, and Peter Omlor in the Department of Registrar; Elizabeth Addison, Deputy Director for Marketing and Communications; Alexandra Partow and Jessica Ferraro in Communications; John Calvelli and Ed Pusz in Graphics; James Gundell, Seth Adleman, and Liz Reddisch in Sales and Marketing; the entire staff of the Exhibition Design and Production department, especially Jerome Neuner and Mark Steigelman for their continually outstanding organization ability; in the Department of Publications, Michael Maegraith, Publisher, Nancy Kranz, Manager, Promotion and Special Services, and Marc Sapir, Production Manager; Susan Richmond, for proofreading; and in the Department of Architecture and Design, Luisa Lorch, Curbie Oestreich, and Abby Pervil for many of the details that could have easily been overlooked.

At The Saint Louis Art Museum we would like to give particular thanks to James D. Burke, Director, and Sidney Goldstein, Associate Director, for encouraging this project. We would also like to thank Jeanette Fausz, Director of Exhibitions; Zoe Perkins, Textile Conservator; Susan Rowe and Carol Kickham for their dependable, good-natured assistance; Rita Wells, Director of Retail Sales; Jim Weidman and Judy Wilson in Development; Cathryn Goodwin in Information Services; Mary Ann Steiner and Patricia Woods in Publications; Registrars Nick Ohlman, Diane Vandegrift, and Bonnie Walker; Jeff Wamhoff, Installation Designer; Dan Esarey and Larry Heberholt in Building Operations; and members of the Program Team—Louise Cameron, Judy Mann, Kay Porter, Dan Reich, Rochelle Steiner, and Mary Susman.

Several people worked enthusiastically to produce the catalogue. In particular we would like to thank Jasmine Moorhead who skillfully organized and edited the manuscripts. We are also grateful to Harriet S. Bee for overseeing the publication and Christopher Zichello for his superb ability to assure the finest quality production. Karin Willis's photographs captured the spirit of the works, and Patrick Seymour, with Ji Lee, created the elegant book design. Finally, we are grateful to all who have participated in and supported this project over the years.

Cara McCarty and **Matilda McQuaid**

Texturing Life

by Cara McCarty

Textiles are among the oldest and most pervasive art forms. Because they are integral to people's lives in innumerable ways and because they can be made of virtually any material, they continue to provide artists and designers with opportunities for imagination and inspiration. This age-old endeavor is reaffirmed by contemporary Japanese textiles, some of the most ingenious and dynamic artifacts being made today. Their beauty and intriguing mysterious qualities are rooted not only in Asian traditions but also in surprising new technical innovations that introduce unsuspected discoveries. Their materials range from ethereal silk, whose atmospheric, vapor-like strands resemble wisps of air, to immutable stainless-steel threads.

Art, interior design, and fashion are the primary areas of textile activity. Many of the artists, employing traditional weaving and dyeing methods and natural or synthetic materials, shape unique works that are either flat or sculptural. By contrast, the fabric designers collaborate with dyers, weavers, and manufacturers, using complex technologies and innovative manipulation techniques to create new textures, finishing processes, and extraordinary visual effects that are then industrially produced. Their textiles are used for residential and commercial interiors, fashion, and practical applications. All of these works, however, are outgrowths of the rich Japanese traditions of spinning, dyeing, weaving, manipulating, shaping, and finishing fabric.

Throughout their history the Japanese have shown great sensitivity toward nature and love for its beauty. Japan's indigenous religion, Shinto, centers on the worship of and communion with the spirits of nature. This, coupled with the country's paucity of natural resources, has instilled in its people a heightened respect for all materials, natural or synthetic. An ability to maximize limited resources and to revere the inherent character of materials is a deeply embedded aspect of Japanese culture.

The Kyoto region and islands of Okinawa (fig. 1) are long-standing cultural and textile centers and harbor many of the artists working with natural fibers. Some of these artists live a hermetic existence in isolated areas, unifying the rural atmosphere where they live with their work. They do not seek publicity or public relations agencies to promote their art. All live in harmony with their surroundings, embracing the elements, working with natural materials, using their hands for repetitive, labor-intensive tasks. They master their chosen techniques, with no arbitrary changes made merely for the sake of innovation. Using natural indigo (*ai*), banana fiber (*basho-fu*), or silk (*kinu*), which have been the mainstays of this craft for centuries, these artists have dedicated their lives to refining their procedures with dignity in a spirit of artistry.

Chiyoko Tanaka, for example, creates surfaces with subtle nuances in grains and colors that are akin to unglazed ceramics. She dyes her warp and weft, then rubs the woven cloth with stones, bricks, or soil in a grinding motion to give them a time-weathered appearance, removing sections much like painters do when scraping off paint, giving each of her unique pieces depth and texture (plates 55, 56). Like stone-washed jeans or aged silk this time-worn quality makes the works particularly intimate. The Maki sisters, Chiaki and Kaori, collaborate and share an entrancing reverence for dyeing and combining silk and linen threads of different textures and origins (fig. 2). Their exquisite palette of earth tones and delicate weaves yield patterns of hypnotic beauty (plates 12, 13).

The astounding variety of industrially produced textiles in Japan is possible because of the manufacturing system in place there today. Textiles were one of the first crafts to be industrialized when Japan began to make its transition to a modern state at the end of the last century. Since then the country has engaged in a relentless process of modernization

Opposite: Detail of pleated fabric from Inoue Pleats Company

and marketing, establishing a solid network of industries with efficient factories that have been the foundation of their economic success. These manufacturers have not only invested in industrialization but have encouraged experimentation, which allows them to abandon false starts and try new ones with a high ratio of success. The current experimental fervor in Japan can be likened to postwar Italy in the 1950s and 1960s, when close collaborations between manufacturers and designers, eager to test new materials and construction techniques, led to an impressive output of original furniture and product forms. This flexibility contrasts with the assembly-line format of mass production in which economic incentives, standardization, and sheer volume virtually prohibit experimentation or customized production.

Although large powerful factories, such as Toray Industries, are technically advanced and automated, the majority, like Kaneko Orimono, Mitasho, Inoue Pleats, and S. Yoshimura, are small and simple by comparison (fig. 3). Many of these Japanese textile factories formerly made kimonos and other garments and have existed for generations. Each one tends to specialize in a technique—cutting, chemical etching, wave-reed weaving, pleating, or flocking, for example—but they take pride in the challenge of developing a new process or texture.

Most of these industrial textiles originate as pristine expanses of glossy polyester. Like a blank sheet of paper, polyester offers virtually limitless possibilities. Once considered an inferior fiber for clothing and furnishings, its status has been elevated through constant reinvention and forward thinking. This prosaic fabric has been enlivened by texturing its surface, an approach often used to conceal defects in lesser-grade plastics or glass. Heating, steaming, puncturing, dissolving with acid, polishing, clipping, shaving—abusive treatments associated with durable materials like stone, ceramics, or glass—transform polyester into cloth that challenges our notion of what textiles can be. Tidy folds, pleats, or crumpled textures are indelibly "baked" into these synthetic fabrics, whose thermoplastic properties have a "memory" for heat (fig. 4). Their variegated textures are characteristic of the Japanese predilection for elegant imperfection and asymmetry found in most of their art forms.

Many Tokyo-based designers have excelled at transforming these mundane materials, like polyester, into magical surfaces with great finesse. They experiment with various fibers and finishing processes to explore a material's physical characteristics often giving new interpretations to such ancient techniques as felting, embroidery, or quilting. Like their counterparts in rural areas they, too, draw on their surroundings for inspiration, but their environment is the raw urban landscape. The character of their textiles reflects the frenzy, glitter, motion, and excitement of city life, charged with

1. Okinawa landscape

2. Chiaki Maki winding yarn

energy. They adopt forms or imagery from manmade products: plastic photo-ID containers or bubble wrap, for instance. Other times, their works represent abstractions of natural forces—decay, weathering, renewal. For some, like the pioneering and influential team of Issey Miyake and Makiko Minagawa of Miyake Design Studio (plates 57–62) or Reiko Sudo of Nuno Corporation, recycling and reuse of materials are prime concerns. Rusted nails and barbed wire become lyrical sources of poetic inspiration for Sudo's Scrapyard series (plate 22).

These visionary designers incorporate both ancient methods and experimental technologies into their untypical ways of working with textiles. They transfigure flat cloth into bas relief by manipulating it chemically or burning out sections; yarns with opposing characteristics are juxtaposed to create the equivalent of lace; acids are used to stretch or shrink separate networks of threads, creating a blistered texture. They weave windows and holes into fabric and steam-heat it, creating distorted, feltlike surfaces and perforated cloth. They have explored the potentials of reflective surfaces of metallics and polyester slit films. In some cases this revolutionary treatment of textiles and fashion has not only reshaped the look of the body and the way people dress but has also redefined the way they walk and move (fig. 5). It is this type of intelligent playing that is forging original works, new discoveries, and modes of expression specific to our era.

Sometimes, artists and designers have spawned new textile products by appropriating manufacturing processes developed for industrial purposes totally unrelated to the textile field. For instance, at the joint instigation of American artist Sheila Hicks and Junichi Arai, who were searching for a fireproof material to create a monumental stage curtain (fig. 6), engineers at Bridgestone Metalpha Corporation in Tochigi developed a new product using stainless-steel fiber (plate 14). Further collaborations between Arai and a Pachinko parlor-game-machine engineer focused on making stainless-steel threads elastic by plying and twisting them so they could be woven on mechanized looms without breaking. Sudo worked with an automobile manufacturer to apply the spattering technology used for polishing automobile hardware to coat her fabric with a silky stainless-steel finish (plate 19).

More direct cross-seminations can be found between the textile and paper industries. Historically, these industries were often located within the same village, and both were linked to kimono making. Increasingly today, textile and paper factories may be found under the same roof, particularly in the Fukui prefecture, where combining paper with synthetic threads has become a specialty. Paper has been traditionally used for clothing because it is surprisingly warm, durable, and astonishingly water-resistant. Like textiles, numerous textures and surfaces can be achieved in

3. Inoue Pleats Company, Ltd., Tokyo

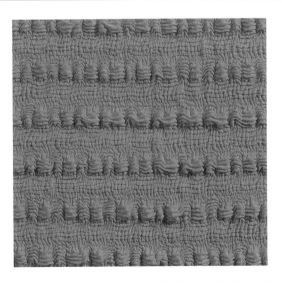

4. Detail of pleated fabric from Inoue Pleats Company

paper by mixing various types of pulp, bark, and plants. Paper, with interlocking fibers that entangle and mesh, may even be dyed like fabric. Various types are likened to linen, cotton, and silk—materials that wear well, are soft to the touch, and are lustrous and smooth. Given the inherent similarities between the two materials it is not surprising that a number of fabrics incorporate paper or are processed to resemble *washi*, Japanese handmade paper. Current practices of heating, shriveling, and crumpling textiles softens them and gives them crinkled, paperlike textures and sounds. Several designers even manipulate fabric using origami paper molds. Cloth sandwiched between geometric, puzzle-like forms are vacuum-set in high temperature presses. Even when the folds are pulled open the works always return to their original angular shapes as with origami (plate 45).

The role of cloth continues to expand as highly specialized textiles are being engineered for particular needs. Spurred by the search for new markets and an acknowledgment of the world's finite resources, some Japanese textile manufacturers are turning their attention to such pervasive health and environmental issues as allergies, skin diseases, radiation from computers, and land erosion. In an effort to control the temperature of highways, they have begun to line roads with fabric that can be "plugged in" to heat the icy pavement. Because of the versatility that can be achieved with their durable structures, the functional properties of their

fibers, their manipulability—rigid to pliable, molded, or sculpted—and their thickness, textiles will play an even larger role in our lives in the future.

Contemporary Japanese textiles are enmeshed in one of the key design issues of our time—the reconciliation of craft and the look of the handmade within a rapidly changing technological society that depends on mass production. Their rich tactile and sensual qualities rely on the crossover applications between craft, art, and industry: very few can be considered *tour de force* engineering achievements alone. While the industrial process is the vehicle of expression for many of the designers, the ultimate impact is dependent on some handwork. Computer-driven mechanized looms are routinely interrupted so that tiny elements, like feathers or paper, can be inserted by hand. The abundance of slick, mass-produced objects and the dearth of tactile sensation in our lives make us crave unique objects that bear the poetic and meaningful mark of the hand. This perhaps explains the worldwide resurgence in textile making today. Finding ways to preserve the individuality and diversity that is a hallmark of small-scale production while simultaneously maintaining a high level of output is a challenge in a world that has become increasingly standardized.

Although these textiles have clear antecedents in Japanese craft traditions that have been evolving for centuries, their fresh spirit and unconventional techniques and materials make them peculiar to our time, to our sensibility. Art is not always about

5. Runway photograph of Issey Miyake's *Prism* series

6. Sheila Hicks, *Doncho* (stage curtain), Kiryu City Cultural Center, 1997

denying and rebelling against traditions; it can be part of a lifelong quest for harmony. Japan's natural isolation as an island, reinforced by prolonged periods of self-imposed seclusion, permitted it to develop a distinct cultural style and a strong sense of national identity that continues to this day. Perhaps for these reasons Japanese artists and designers seem to be comfortable with their traditions: maintaining the spirit of a Japanese sensibility, while redefining and updating it without imitating the past. Some of the processes may be viewed as shortcuts from labor-intensive methods, but the practice of manipulating and imposing structure on cloth, inspired by traditional *shibori* techniques, has a long history in Japanese culture (fig. 7). Tradition and crafts represent a continuum, a link to one's cultural heritage, but they are also sources of inspiration, giving one the tools to move forward. For cultures to mature and to further develop this continuity, an homage to tradition paired with an optimism for the future must prevail. As with these artists and designers and their textiles, the result is the creation of a new aesthetic.

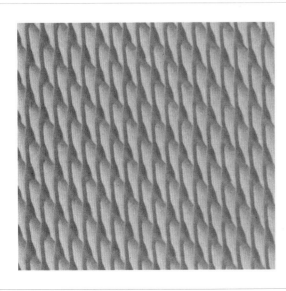

7. Detail of pleated fabric from
Inoue Pleats Company

Transformations:
Process and Technique in Contemporary Japanese Textiles

by Matilda McQuaid

Change and the accommodation of new technology to traditional creative methods pose a challenge for contemporary life. Most of the world's cultures have been confronted with a merging of ancient techniques and twentieth-century industry. Textiles have not been exempt from this phenomenon; as they are inextricably linked to daily activities and language, they provide an exemplary medium in which to examine this integration of old and new. In Japan a particularly rich textile tradition has been transformed into one of the most innovative industries in the field. Factories five or more generations old, which used to specialize in some aspect of kimono production, now develop materials and technologies that contribute significantly to the contemporary textile culture. Ancestral techniques have not been replaced but adapted and expanded so that the kimono, for example, has remained a symbolic unit of measure for cloth, like the tatami for Japanese architecture.

The collection of truly remarkable fabrics presented here may look strangely new, but some of their processes can be traced back for centuries and evidence a thorough knowledge by their makers of traditional Japanese textiles. Their transformation into models of contemporary design is most pronounced in the use of different and new materials, and in surface articulation. The qualities that make these textiles such eye-catching revelations are defined by the primary process by which each work was conceived. To create a fabric that has the translucency of a spider's web or the reflective capabilities of metal or the fractured surface of wrinkled paper requires the creator to have not only a fertile imagination but an expertise in using twentieth-century tools and technology.

These works are organized into six categories that describe the predominant characteristic of each: TRANSPARENT, DYED, REFLECTIVE, PRINTED, SCULPTED, LAYERED. The grouping of a textile into one category does not preclude its relevance in another. Some of these fabrics, for example, may rely on a printing technique to achieve a three-dimensional relief or a layering process to produce a shimmering metallic surface. The divisions serve only as a structure enabling alternative journeys of discovery and a guide to creative processes that have transformed flat planes into incredible inventions in cloth.[1]

TRANSPARENT

Transparency implies both a literal and metaphorical lightness. This lightness can be achieved through the blending of different fibers, especially with the advent of new synthetic yarns. Or, in other cases, this quality has been the hallmark of centuries-old traditional methods that use only organic materials. From the handwoven to high-tech, remote islands to densely-populated industrial cities, artists are fascinated by the mystique of the transparent.

A tradition that almost became extinct after World War II was the making of *basho-fu*, or banana fiber cloth, which is particular to the Okinawan prefecture, a group of islands known as the "kingdom of dyeing and weaving." *Basho-fu* is born of Okinawa's tropical climate and landscape.[2] It has a cooling sensation next to the skin and, rather than clinging to the body, allows air to circulate. The process of spinning and weaving *basho-fu* is extremely laborious and takes years to learn.

Basho-fu is made from the fibers in the heart of the *basho* plant. After the plant has been harvested (fig. 1), the fibers are pulled away from the stalk, bundled, and boiled in water with wood ash. They are then rinsed, weighted with stones, and hung to dry. The fiber is pulled through bamboo tongs that remove any short ends (fig. 2). Fiber strips are only as long as the plant stalk so they are joined by splitting the fibers to the desired diameter (sometimes finer than silk) and tying them with a weaver's knot. The fiber is spun and then carefully twisted, after which it is drawn onto skeins to equalize tension (fig. 3). It is then ready for dyeing and patterning. Pervasive in Okinawa is the dyeing technique *kasuri*, meaning "to blur," where the warp and/or weft yarns are partially bound or compressed before dyeing. *Basho-fu* designs are often taken from pattern books that have been passed down for several generations. These books contain textile samples whose richly colored abstract shapes have very specific meanings in the symbolic reading of the cloth.

The dyeing alone takes infinite patience and a considerable amount of time, but it is also affected by fluctuations in temperature and humidity so the whole process becomes dependent upon the environment. After additional stages of boiling, rinsing, scouring, and airing, the final sheen of the work is enhanced by rubbing a porcelain teacup over the surface of the fabric. Considering it takes twenty days to tie enough fiber for one kimono, it is amazing that this labor-intensive process has survived.

In the village of Kijoka, the weaver Toshiko Taira (fig. 4) has a studio that is the principal source for *basho-fu* in Japan. In her atelier, which has been designated an Intangible Cultural Asset, or Living National Treasure, approximately thirty women are engaged in the preparatory stages of thread making, while another forty women weave. Taira, like other *basho-fu* artists, chooses to teach

the next generation the methods that were handed down to her and avoids shortcuts that will lead to the detriment of these highly acquired skills for the sake of a temporary expedient.[3] Akiko Ishigaki, who lives on one of the southern-most islands of Okinawa, perpetuates the timeless craft in the same spirit. If Taira helped to revive interest in *basho-fu*, then Ishigaki has contemporized it by combining it with other materials such as silk and *choma*, or China grass—a process called *gumbo*—making it accessible to a wider audience.

Ishigaki believes that "a piece of woven fabric not only protects or decorates the human body but is also important for costumes used for ritual praying and dancing in the annual religious festivals,"[4] which are at the core of the island's tradition of honoring the cycle of life. All steps of making cloth are tied to nature's cycles: in spring, Ishigaki grows *basho*, *choma*, and silk cocoons; in summer, she collects bark, fruits, and roots for dyeing these materials. Weaving the fibers is done on days when she cannot work outside and the climate is suitable for weaving: high humidity is the most desirable. One of the most beautiful aspects of this process is seeing the cloth (plate 2) when it is washed in the sea, an act that not only stabilizes the dye but reinforces its poetic connection to the land and water from which it was created.

Another Okinawan weaver is Michiko Uehara, who uses silk exclusively. She uses the thinnest yarn possible, sometimes as fine as 6.4 deniers.[5]

1. Akiko and Kinsei Ishigaki cutting *basho*, Okinawa, 1997

2. Akiko Ishigaki stripping *basho* to make thread, Okinawa, 1997

Uehara describes this thread, so thin it is almost imperceptible, as "weaving air" or *akezuba ori* — the weave of a dragonfly's wings. In **Yuyake (Evening Glow)** (plate 7), a double weave, the floating warp threads reveal the incredible delicacy of the yarn. The thin, green color yarn of **Sogen (Grassy Plains)** (plate 7) is reminiscent of algae that cover rocks underneath the sea. Uehara uses only natural dyes derived from plants such as *fukugi* (yellow), logwood (brown), *annatto* (yellow-red), madder (purple-red), gromwell (purple), and indigo (blue). Her title **Tobi Gasuri (Alternating Kasuri)** (fig. 5; plate 6) is a reference to the *kasuri* technique used to dye the warp and weft threads with *fukugi* and *annatto*, which when combined become a glowing golden color.

Reiko Sudo, who works as the chief designer for Nuno Corporation in Tokyo, derives her ideas as much from industrial production as from nature and tradition. The loving and attentive care of Uehara's creations makes a striking contrast to Sudo's seemingly aggressive approach to creating a fabric with a similar cloudlike transparency. In **Stratus** (plate 1), Sudo creates a fabric with a wispy quality inspired by traditional resist-dyeing techniques such as *katazome*, or screen resist, and *tsutsu-gaki*, or line-drawing resist. She has developed a personal method using transparent silk organdy that she paints with starch-resist then immerses in calcium nitrate, which causes the exposed "dyed" areas to crimp and bunch into opaque clumps. The resist-covered areas retain their painted patterns in the original base

cloth. Sudo's **Shutter** (plate 4) alters our ideas about embroidery, traditionally an additive process. In this example, meandering strips of nylon tape are sewn onto a soluble-base fabric that is then dissolved. What is left behind are calligraphic lines or colored tendrils that the designer claims were inspired by rolling steel shutters on storefronts and which have "a certain forlorn *sabi* beauty."

The Sakai brothers of Sakase Adtech Company in Fukui design and produce technical textiles that have specific industrial applications. These may ultimately be concealed in consumer products (such as carbon fiber in golf club shafts) and are considered non-decorative. Qualities of lightness and delicacy do not diminish the strength of these particular fabrics, achieved through a revolutionary weaving process called triaxial weaving (plate 3), in which three yarns—two warp and one weft—are interlaced at sixty- to seventy-degree angles. Resembling a basket weave, the triaxial structure allows maximum flexibility and provides the strength rather than the actual material. The construction also requires less raw material and therefore is lighter than conventionally woven fabrics.

NASA developed this triaxial structure in the late 1960s to fill the needs of space scientists for a dimensionally stable and lightweight fabric to be used in aeronautics. This "invention," however, had been preceded more than 1,200 years before, during the Nara period (710–794 A.D.), by a version of this triaxial structure called *ra*, examples of which

3. Spools of *basho* thread

4. Toshiko Taira in her studio, 1997

are preserved in the Shosoin Temple repository in Nara. Woven on a handloom and a room-size industrial loom (fig. 6) respectively, *ra* and triaxial weaving both utilize the idea of a warp thread running diagonally instead of vertically, allowing the textile to be stretched in all directions without causing stress at any point. The triaxial material has been used to make antenna reflectors, solar panels, skis, fishing rods, speaker cones, and medical supports for people who suffer from joint deficiency.

The **Encircling Fishing Net** (plate 5) manufactured by one of the largest textile companies in the world, Toray Industries in Tokyo, must also be light and strong given its end use. Made of Teteron polyester, the net has the ability to expand from 1 1/2 to 132 inches and weighs almost nothing. Instead of knots, this net is held together using a twist technique developed in the early part of this century and modernized here with polyester yarns that are interlocked to form a mesh, then heat-treated to eliminate distortions and create a flattened surface. The technique has proven extremely effective in offering low water-resistance, ease in maneuvering and storage because of less bulk, and greater strength than a knotted net. It also prevents bruising of the fish, which is important to a culture that relies on presentation—be it of food or tea or flowers—to assure a harmonious ensemble.

DYED

The subtle variation of color achieved by dyeing in contemporary Japanese textiles is a pure revelation. Dyers have an almost spiritual devotion to transforming yarn or cloth into extensions of their perceptions of earth, water, and sky through color. Walks through woods and along streams can result in great discoveries for Chiaki and Kaori Maki who use natural dyes and dyeing processes to produce an endless variety of subtle hues and tones with an irregular and unpredictable beauty directly connected with nature (fig. 7). They have found that both large and small acts can affect the ultimate outcome or appearance of cloth—from seasonal changes to a specific type of dye to a calculated twist of the yarn. The Maki sisters use a computer-driven handloom for design experimentation before determining how to produce their ideas in series. In **Hollow Bamboo** (plate 13), tassar silk, woven by hand on a four-harness loom, has been given a soft twisting in the spinning process and is combined with malda silk that has been dyed with the natural dyes of anar and harad.[6] Similarly, in **Flux** (plate 12), woven on a ten-harness loom, three different types of silks—malda, dupion, and tassar—are dyed with indigo and anar. For **Capriccio** (plate 12), a malda and tassar silk and wool combination creates different densities causing the fabric to be alternately transparent and opaque. The natural colors of the tassar silk and wool offset the malda silk that

5. Michicko Uehara holding a variation of **Tobi Gasuri (Alternating Kasuri)**, 1997

6. Triaxial weaving machine, Fukui

has been dyed with harad. The Makis reserve the final finishing stage of the cloth for the wearer, who conditions and enhances it by touch and handling.

No other color is more associated with Japan than the deep blue of *ai*, or indigo. Introduced from South China in the eighth century, the indigo plant was grown widely in Japan and soon became the most sought after dyestuff. It was not unusual for villages to have a specialized indigo dyer to meet the demands of the local population. As a young man, Hiroyuki Shindo was enraptured by the magical colors achieved from natural indigo and was equally saddened by the decline in the number of *aishi*, or indigo growers, and processors who supplied it to the artisans. He determined to revive and transform this craft of working with natural indigo that had almost vanished in modern Japan. He sunk ceramic dye pots into the earthen floor of his thatched-roof studio/farmhouse in the mountains north of Kyoto and began dyeing. The dried indigo leaves, called *sukumo*, are converted into dyestuff by the addition of lye, lime, wheat bran, sake, and a microorganism. The lye comes from ash accumulated in his wood-burning stoves, and both the ash and *sukumo* are later used to fertilize his garden. Fermentation takes a week to ten days, and the indigo dyestuff must be stirred regularly. Indigo microbes survive best at a temperature of twenty degrees centigrade, so the indigo pots are heated with charcoal throughout the winter. Shindo's art and life remain inextricably linked to nature.

Shindigo Square Series 92-1 (plates 10, 11) is composed of five narrow kimono-width handwoven *asa*, or hemp panels, with uneven selvages and a rough surface. To guide the dyeing, Shindo bastes a square outline in the center of the five panels. Parallel to his dye vat, he suspends the cloth slung on a frame so that its middle drapes closest to the dye; using a level, he raises one end of the frame about two centimeters above the other while it is dipped, which facilitates the gradational dyeing effect. Indigo takes on its full intensity through repeated dipping and subsequent oxidization, therefore color is not a result of the time submerged in the dye but how many times it has been dipped. During the course of three days, a piece may be dyed fifty times. Barely visible, the horizontal lines from the gradation technique document the transformative and cumulative dyeing process.

Shindo explains his **Space Panel** (fig. 8) with the word *okkochi* which means "the eastern wind" and when spoken also suggests "to let fall." It describes a kind of dyeing technique developed in Arimatsu (near Nagoya) about 300 years ago during the Edo period. The story of its origin claims that a wind from the east blew just a corner of kimono fabric into a vat of indigo. From this incident, a new kind of shaped dyeing was born that was less methodical than traditional *shibori* tie-dye resist and more reflective of the patterns of nature. In Shindo's *okkochi* interpretation, he makes a wooden trough about four centimeters deep and scatters small

7. Chiaki Maki and Akiko Ishigaki dyeing cloth, Okinawa, 1997

8. Hiroyuki Shindo. Space Panel. 1993. Cotton and hemp. Handwoven and *okkochi* dyed with indigo, 48¾ x 74" (123.8 x 188 cm). Collection Sheila Hicks

stones and pebbles on the bottom and at the edges. Laying the cloth in this shallow trough he carefully pushes it into the concave shapes in-between the stones. Dye is ladled many times into the depressions of the fabric, and he constantly changes the boundary of the well and the depth of the stones to make gradations of color. The free-form clouds that are achieved have been carefully created through his faithful attention and joyful play. The effect of seeing these panels is like entering an indigo sky.

The artist Jun Tomita uses the traditional dyeing technique of *kasuri*, the Japanese word for *ikat*. (*Ikat* is derived from the Malay-Indonesian word *mengikat* meaning "to tie or to bind.") *Kasuri* has been popular in Japan since the seventeenth century; *ikat* was established much earlier, but was used only in very special circumstances on clothing worn mainly by the aristocracy. There are many classifications of *kasuri*, according to which threads are dyed with respect to their function in the weaving process. In **Kasuri Panel 151–1** (plates 8, 9), only the warp threads have been bound and dyed, making it a *warp kasuri*. As Tomita handweaves, a blurring occurs at the junction of different colors, almost impossible to achieve had it been applied as brushwork, and creating subtleties of colors within colors that are only revealed by close scrutiny. The beauty in the work lies in the variations of tone and the soft lines that seem to emanate from each boundary of color.

REFLECTIVE

Reflective surfaces can be achieved in a variety of ways—from technical dyeing process to the use of actual metallic yarns.[7] Historically, metal-leafed paper would be twisted around an inner silk or paper yarn to form the metallic thread that was then woven into or embroidered on a cloth surface. The metallic leaf could also be applied directly to fill areas between the heavily embroidered motifs.

In the twentieth century, with the advent of synthetic fibers, there are less expensive ways to make metallic yarns. One can sandwich metal such as aluminum foil between layers of clear film—the exact process used in making audiocassette tapes. The most commonly used method now consists of a single-ply polyester film that is metallicized on one side by means of a vacuum deposit of aluminum. A clear or tinted lacquer is applied to both sides of the film and then slit into thin strips to make a kind of thread called polyester slit film. Japan is the largest producer of this yarn in the world.

Junichi Arai has turned slit film into astounding and animated textiles. He began weaving with metallic fibers in the mid-1950s and has obtained numerous patents for inventions that employ this unique thread (fig. 9). A process called "melt-off," for example, requires dissolving the metallic thread to leave behind a transparent cloth, and "burn-out" inverts this process by leaving behind the metal grid. **Moon Light** (plate 15) and **Deep Sea** (plate 16) are

9. Junichi Arai in his studio, Kiryu, 1997

dazzling examples of this innovative technology and have had fashion applications. Before Arai begins the "melt-off" process in **Moon Light**, he uses *shibori*, which comes from the word *shiboru* meaning "to wring, squeeze, or press."[8] Certain parts are wrapped in order to retain metallic areas when dyeing the cloth. Using a weft yarn of sirofil, a "new generation wool" that contains ten percent nylon filament, with *shibori* and the "melt-off" process, Arai discovered it was possible to create a velvetlike texture. In **Deep Sea**, a woven polyester and aluminum fabric is subjected to "melt-off" and then to heat-transfer printing, which is normally used to transfer designs and colors to the surface of a fabric by high temperature (200 degrees centigrade). Exposing the fabric numerous times to this transfer print process, extraordinary patterns and textures can accumulate successively with overlapping layers of color and permanently pleated wrinkles. The impetus for this highly technical procedure is purely aesthetic—creating a textured fabric of emerald green and sapphire blue reminiscent of the East China Sea.

Arai calls himself a "textile planner" and "an experienced hunter of knowledge" and works in both ancient and explorative technologies. Free from traditional boundaries, he enjoys collaborating with textile engineers and being challenged by designers to find solutions for specific projects. For instance, he worked with artist Sheila Hicks to find new fade-resistant and fireproof materials to be used for a *doncho*, or stage curtain. He followed through on this project with the development and research team of Masami Kikuchi and Tatsuo Hirayama of the Bridgestone Metalpha Corporation, which specializes in tire manufacturing and top-level metal technology. They came up with a revolutionary fiber that could be woven into cloth but also has characteristics inherent to stainless steel including strength and durability. A composite wire rod 5.5 millimeters in diameter comprised of 1,700 iron-clad stainless-steel filaments is gradually drawn or stretched over many stages. It is crucial not to break any of the filaments so that when the iron cladding is removed by acid, the filaments can be processed into a mass of continuing fiber (tow), finally becoming aligned strands of yarn. One of the most innovative features of this material, marketed as Alphatex™ (plate 14), is its ability to take on color without being dyed using a combination of chemical and heat processes. Through a careful manipulation of temperature, the steel thread can achieve rich hues. Virtually all stages of manufacture are performed by robotic technology, with only occasional maintenance visits by humans. Fashion designer Yoshiki Hishinuma is one of the first to use it in clothing, where it is, appropriately, spot-welded rather than sewn (fig. 10).

Koichi Yoshimura, a designer and manufacturer in Fukui, collaborated with Issey Miyake and Makiko Minagawa, two of the most eminent figures in the textile and fashion industry, to produce a reflective fabric without employing any kind of metallic yarn. Later, Yoshimura further developed

10. Arai (right) supervising cloth being spot-welded, 1997

this process with Reiko Sudo to make **Blue Mirror Cloth with Wrinkles** (plate 17) and added wrinkles to emphasize its texture and reflective capabilities. It is satin-backed, meaning that it is a two-faced fabric with dull and lustrous sides. Instead of the customary silk or rayon used in satin-backing, it is the polyester monofilament (commonly used for fishing line) which Yoshimura substitutes in the weft that provides its shiny surface. When Makiko Minagawa commissioned a fabric from Yoshimura that would look like "light reflecting on the surface of calm water," the result was **Iridescent Satin** (plate 18). Yoshimura uses a satin weave with polyester filament and cotton that is piece-dyed after weaving, creating a multicolored fabric whose variations depend on light and viewing angle.

Reiko Sudo's **Copper Cloth** (fig. 11; plate 20) has a radiant quality that is a result of using a weft of copper wire—the same material used in telephone lines—that has been coated with polyurethane to prevent brittleness and discoloration. The white warp thread is a recently invented fiber called Promix™. Architect Toyo Ito has found this fabric particularly suitable for interior environments because it retains its shape when crumpled or draped.

Sudo's fabric achieves an almost liquid state in **Stainless Steel Gloss** (plate 19), a metal-coated woven polyester. It is polished by a calender, a factory-size ironing machine, which flattens the fabric or embosses it. After this stage, three powdered metals—chrome, nickel, and iron (the components of stainless steel)—are "spatter-plated" separately onto the polyester to impart a shiny stainless-steel finish. This spatter-plating is a technology used in the automobile industry to apply metallic finishes to automotive trim. Differences in weave density and surface texture allow for a wide range of lusters, many of them yet to be explored.

PRINTED

The tradition of printing has always involved the mechanical transferring of characters or patterns to a surface, using inked type, blocks, or plates. Immediate associations with the technique in Japan are the two-dimensional representational images of the landscape or plants and flowers that adorn clothing. Conventionally the process has a visual rather than tactile effect. Expectations about printing are drastically altered, however, when one discovers that printing inks have been replaced by chemicals and adhesives. In Sudo's **Scattered Rubber Bands** (plate 24), acrylic and silicone provide the medium with which to reinterpret this motif on cloth. Stacks of freshly fired bricks are the point of departure for Keiji Otani's **Brickyard** (fig. 12; plate 21), a two-way, knitted-nylon base fabric printed with polyurethane foam. The pattern of the bricks remains in relief even when the cloth is stretched to its full extent.

In Sudo's Scrapyard series, barbed wire, nails, and iron plates are recycled and weathered to

11. Detail of **Copper Cloth**

12. Detail of **Brickyard**

become the printing tool for the cloth. In the case of **Scrapyard (Nail)** (plate 22), nails that have been treated with iron oxide (rusted), are laid on top of a dampened rayon fabric until a trace is imprinted (fig. 13). Different patterns can be formed simply by varying the placement of the metal scraps and the length of the weathering time.

Sudo's inspiration for **Graffiti** (plate 23) are the markings found on an earthen wall in Anatolia, Turkey, which she translates into a pattern on cloth (fig. 14). Using a method called flocking, a binder (adhesive) is first screenprinted on top of a polyester organdy base, and tiny rayon or nylon fibers (0.5–1 millimeter long) are affixed to the base fabric and made to stand on end by using an electric charge. Flocking is an inexpensive way to simulate velvets or other raised-surface materials, but in **Graffiti** the technique takes on a renewed elegance when juxtaposed with a transparent gossamer fabric.

SCULPTED

Any material that has the ability to be molded or shaped in a particular way can be sculpted—stone is chiseled, metal is cast, clay is thrown or modeled. When cloth surfaces are sculpted, highly articulated, individual landscapes are formed by manipulating and revealing the inner behavior of the yarns. Heat plays an instrumental role, and many sculpted fabrics are, in fact, baked. They are often printed with or adhered to a heat-responsive substance that

will determine the final outcome of the texture.

Wave Process Velvet (plate 48) by Masaji Yamazaki and **Jellyfish** (plate 46) by Sudo use a process in which an industrial vinyl polychloride, originally developed for automobile upholstery and with a preset fifty percent heat-shrinkage ratio, is partially layered either on polyester/rayon velvet (Yamazaki) or on a polyester fabric (Sudo) by screenprinting. It is then flash heated. This causes the velvet or the polyester to shrivel where the vinyl adheres (fig. 15). Because synthetics such as polyester have thermoplastic characteristics, or the ability to be molded permanently by heat, each fabric retains the bumpy surface after the vinyl polychloride is peeled away. This industrially driven design produces undulating planes of color and texture that mimic the ripple effect often produced by *shibori* dyeing.

In **Epidermis (Ocean)** (plate 36) Yuh Okano achieves a high-relief surface with beads made from urea resin, a substance which can withstand very high temperature. Okano wraps these beads in the polyester fabric and binds them in place with rubber bands. She dyes the fabric then repeats the process making new protuberances of different colors. The cloth is then heat set in order to permanently retain the shapes of the beads, which are then removed and the fabric is washed to remove any impurities collected during the process. With her **Epidermis (Forest)** (plate 37), she inserts metal discs into crepe polyester to supply the shape. Each disc is bound

13. Reiko Sudo with rusted plates used in her Scrapyard series, 1997

14. Reiko Sudo. Study for **Graffiti**. Pencil and watercolor on board. 16½ x 12" (42 x 30.5 cm). Collection Reiko Sudo

and then the fabric is immersed in a dye solution that reaches 100 degrees centigrade, at which point it shrinks. When it is pulled out of the dye solution and unbound, the metal discs are removed and the cloth is heat pressed at 180 degrees centigrade to flatten the protuberances. The shapes become stiff but maintain the form of the discarded metal discs.

There are three types of pleating processes: manual pleating—pleats are pressed by hand with an iron; machine pleating—parallel pleats are made by running a bolt of fabric between heated rollers and creating a knife-edged pleat; and hand pleating—precut fabric is sandwiched between chemically treated folded paper patterns which are heated to make the pleats. Inoue Pleats Company was the first company to produce pleats on a large scale in Japan. They and, even more, Issey Miyake, have popularized pleats in contemporary fashion worldwide. There are many variations, as in **Wrinkle P** (plate 40), developed by Inoue Company, which is produced by randomly stuffing polyester fabric into a small container and placing it in a thermosetting machine where the pleats are permanently set. Machine and manual pleating are combined to create **Crystal** Σ (plate 39). Vertical pleats are made in the first stage followed by a special manual method that compresses the pleated fabric to a width that is approximately one-third the original size. The result is a transformation from an anonymous polyester to wrinkled skin or, as Sudo describes **Mica** (frontispiece, p. 16; plate 44), a "multilayered 'fool's gold' fabric."

Jürgen Lehl, a Polish-born fashion designer who has lived and worked in Japan for almost thirty years, emphasizes natural materials such as silk, cotton, and wool. His pleating process (plate 28) results from a combination of techniques: twisting the silk threads, basting the pleats, and then setting them with a final steaming. Dyeing takes place at different stages before and after the pleating process. Lehl's ability to empathize and interpret Japanese culture allows his textiles and fashion designs to perpetuate a sensibility associated with Japan.

Pleats can also be produced using a heat-transfer print machine as in Junichi Arai's **Yuragi (Fluctuation)** (plate 27), creating a rustling, crinoline-type fabric, or combining this machine process with a hand-pleating process, as seen in the magical folding and unfolding motion of **Origami Pleat Scarf** (plate 45). This work, designed by Sudo with Mizue Okada, opens to a three-dimensional construction and collapses completely flat at a touch. Its color gradation is achieved by sandwiching colored dye-transfer paper between the fabric and the outer paper during the heat-transfer process.

Urase Company's **Harmony** (cover; fig. 16; plate 47) also holds an element of surprise that, like the pleat scarf, requires human interaction to reveal its secret. As a static piece of cloth it simply looks stylishly wrinkled; however, when the wrinkles are pulled apart, as if to straighten out the cloth, another interior color reveals itself. Heat-transfer

15. Detail of **Wave Process Velvet**

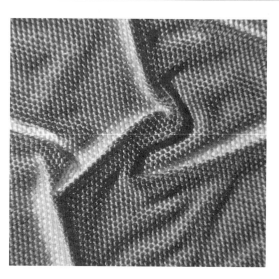

16. Detail of **Harmony**

printing onto an already wrinkled fabric is part of the process, but Shigemi Matsuyama, director of Urase's research and development department, chooses to explain the remaining steps only by citing chemical equations. Urase regularly produces billions of meters of plain polyester, but also works both independently and with outside designers to create innovative new textures and structures.

Mitasho Company in Gumma, a strong member of the Kiryu Textile Union and appreciated for their finely made jacquard fashion fabrics, often collaborates with young designers to develop prototypes. Two of these protégés, Hideko Takahashi and Osamu Mita, share a fascination with disrupting the surface of cloth during and after weaving. Takahashi describes her three-layer **Circle Square II** (plates 34, 35), woven at Mitasho, as a "two-layer cake." She distinguishes the alternating gray-and-white colored layers that comprise the "cake" by cutting weft threads that float above the base cloth. A felting process shrinks the cloth and diminishes its size by twenty percent. The fabric is then acid dyed, causing further shrinkage so that when finished, the length is fifty-three percent and the width thirty-eight percent of the original size. Mita's **Wool Mesh Window** (plates 29, 30) is similar to **Circle Square II** less one layer. The front and back sides of the fabric are of equal importance, one disclosing the ghost of the other. **Stick** (plate 33), which Takahashi describes as "human ribs," is a double cloth whose two layers are woven together at very few junctures. The exterior

texture appears to be hand-appliquéd tubes but is really the top layer of the fabric that has been cut, rolled, stuffed with tulle, and handsewn closed. Each of Takahashi's works is as playful as it is sculptural.

In Japanese culture there is a tendency to express beauty through the combination of different materials, as if the beauty and character of one is only brought out by the other. For instance, the juxtaposition of a highly lacquered surface next to a beautifully granulated ceramic glaze calls attention to the intrinsic smoothness of the former by its contrast to the coarseness of the latter. Mita's **Washi & Wool** (plates 31, 32) attempts a similar opposition using wool and *wa*, a yarn made from a specific type of *washi* paper composed of different fibrous plants such as mulberry and mitsumata. The front side is a plain weave of *washi* that is hollowed out leaving a diamond-shaped wool center, and the back side inverts this construction allowing the weave of the *washi* to form a solid diamond (fig. 17). The fabric is finished in a washer that, as it cleans, shrinks the wool at a different percentage from the *washi*, resulting in a husky textured surface, with the *wa* and wool providing a striking contrast with and a pleasing complement to each other.

Yoshihiro Kimura also combines seemingly disparate material to create an entirely new surface. In **Pedocal** (fig. 18; plate 25), he affixes polyester chiffon to a base of a stretched knitted fabric. An acrylic binder screenprinted in a pattern permeates the fabrics, causing them to join. Rayon fibers are

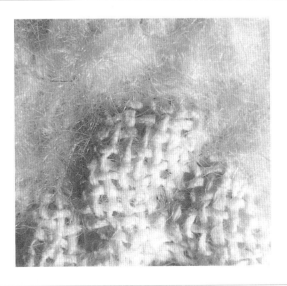

17. Detail of **Washi & Wool**

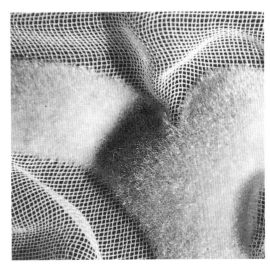

18. Detail of **Pedocal**

affixed to this binder and, using an electric charge (flocking), are made to stand vertically. The knitted fabric that had been stretched during this whole process is loosened again, leaving the double-layered cloth puckered and covered with crevices that resemble a topographical view of the Earth.

This purposeful transformation of cloth into buckled and tufted shapes or into organic textures that appear accidental has been exploited by Junichi Arai in **Charred Fabric** (plate 26). By using a nylon slit-film yarn in the warp and sirofil wool in the weft, binding portions of the base fabric, and felting the cloth, Arai causes the fabric to lose its original shiny surface.

LAYERED

A precedent for layering in Japanese textiles and fashion can be found in the evolution of the kimono when, in extreme cases, especially during the Heian period (794–1185 A.D.), women of high rank wore ten or more layers of robes. The layers varied in cut and color, each carefully chosen to offset and complement one another, with all the superimpositions visible at the neck, front, and sleeve openings. One author writes, "The harmony of the whole was considered one of the most telling indications of a woman's sensibility."[9]

No other fashion and textile design team in Japan has used layering techniques more effectively to create intriguing three-dimensional work than Issey Miyake with Makiko Minagawa. Since 1970 with the founding of Miyake Design Studio, they have transformed fabrics into wearable sculptures. Miyake's work has been exhibited alongside the sculpture of Isamu Noguchi to emphasize not only the three-dimensional quality of each but the shared spirit and sensibility within their chosen mediums. Although Minagawa works closely with Miyake, she prefers to remain in the background and believes that textiles are only part of the equation of fashion. In this relationship, the textile designer, although of utmost importance, supports and makes feasible the concepts of the fashion designer. It is their ongoing dialogue that determines the success of the final garment.

This design dialogue produced Miyake's recent **Prism** series (plates 57–60). These ingenious coats and dresses are layers of materials that combine handwork with a traditional industrial method called needlepunching, customarily used for carpetmaking. Needles punch through a web of materials, thereby entangling and joining the fibers. For the base fabric, lightweight wool is used for the dress and heavier felt for the coat (fig. 19). Subsequently, pieces of different fabrics, such as polyester chiffon and nonwoven batting, are placed on areas of the base cloth that have been prepared for patterning and cutting, creating a collage of materials. All of the fabrics are then joined together with the base cloth by needlepunching, making the collage elements intertwine and become transparent, with only

19. Detail of **Prism** coat

blurred outlines remaining of the original pieces. In order to preserve the beauty of the patterns, the fabric is cut only where it is absolutely necessary. Sometimes the fabric is merely folded and tacked on the reverse, similar to the making of a kimono. Conceptually, this can be considered a recycling process because of its reuse of fabric, and visually, it is like painting: the surface of the garment is built up with layers of color that either blend together or appear as independent blocks.

Miyake's **Star Burst** series (plates 61, 62) exemplifies the metamorphosis that can take place in a simple cotton shirt through layering. The shirt is overlaid with silver and copper foil, heat-pressed, and then pulled at the seams and fold lines, which tears the foil and produces random patterns. The metal lends elegance and luxury to an otherwise plain shirt.

Layering is both an additive and subtractive process as surfaces are constructed and then manually or chemically cut or dissolved to reveal each woven tier. In Sudo's **Patched Paper** (plate 52), Mino washi paper[10] is cut into thin strips using a traditional technique by which gold and silver threads were once made. On a jacquard loom, the paper weft is woven into the polyester warp so that it does not twist or fold. The paper slit yarns are then cut by hand to achieve a random quality. Similarly, Akihiro Kaneko, of the prestigious Kaneko Orimono Company, created **#1926 Brown Hair** (plate 53) by using a jacquard weave with warp yarns of rayon

and cupra and floating acetate weft threads that were then cut after weaving. The tangle of threads on the surface obscures the checkerboard pattern of the true structure of the cloth underneath (fig. 20). **Bark** (plate 54), one of Junichi Arai's most popular and inventive works, is also a jacquard double weave, made of cotton, wool, and Spandex. Felting causes the fabric to become denser and the black-and-white pattern to transform the cloth into a texture that looks like aged wood.

This subtractive process can help to make curious juxtapositions of solid/void and clear/opaque dualities. Sudo creates **Crackle Cloth** (plate 50) by using a polyurethane binder to affix a polyester organdy base to rayon. Parts of the rayon fabric are burned away with an acid that does not affect the polyester. The rayon takes on a tattered appearance leaving the polyester organdy in translucent patterns. This clear and opaque quality has an affinity with Naomi Kobayashi's **Composition Ito-Kukan** (plate 64), a very different work in terms of process but similar in its use of triangular patches to define voids. Kobayashi stretches twisted paper thread around a solid wood frame. Pieces of washi are then randomly pasted on some of the triangular areas formed by the overlap of the threads with konnyaku paste,[11] which helps to solidify the form of the overall work. The frame is removed after the work is stabilized by these areas of washi. The form and the shadows that it casts constantly change depending upon the lighting (fig. 21), and for Kobayashi,

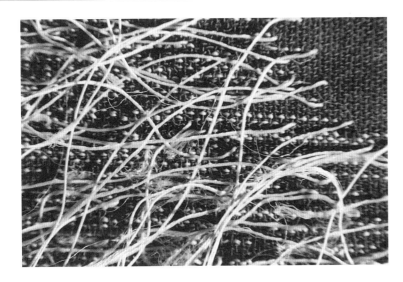

20. Detail of **#1926 Brown Hair**

this communicates "the unity of the never-ending providence of nature, the cycle of life, the eternal cycles of the universe."

Artist Chiyoko Tanaka works alone in a cypress forest on the northern edge of Kyoto. Her **Grinded Fabric—Ocher: RF#4** (plates 55, 56) is made of linen and ramie with applications of *Jurakudai* soil.[12] She coined the phrase "Grinded Fabric" for works where she carefully "polishes" the surfaces. As the artist explains, it is not so much the final color of the surface but the use of a particular stone or brick, that is most important to her. For this panel, Tanaka used a stone to burnish both the front and back so that previously concealed warp threads began to appear on the surface (fig. 22). The ocher color of the square results from carefully rubbing soil onto the surface. By continued pressure and repeated conditioning of the cloth, Tanaka has found that she can satisfactorily transfer the texture of the earth into her canvas.

This peeling away to expose an inner part is the concept of Sudo's **Moss Temple** (plate 51). Velvet cloth is woven to conceal the soft rayon piling of the interior hidden between the outside layers of polyester. A heat-reactive chemical pigment is printed on the polyester, and, when it reaches a temperature of 235 degrees centigrade, the printed area melts off allowing the rayon pile to peek through (fig. 23). The subtractive process Yamazaki and Yoshihiro Kimura use in **Japanese Paper on Velvet** (plate 49) is conceptually similar. They use a polyurethane

binder to affix the *washi* paper to velvet. The two-layer fabric is rinsed with water, and *washi* that has not adhered to the velvet is ultimately washed away. The tattered texture that remains is almost biological in its composition, soft but strangely distant.

Some works by Eiji Miyamoto, Kaneko, and Sudo encase various materials between transparent exterior layers. In **#2765 Yuragi (Fluctuation)** (plate 66), Kaneko constructs a double-face fabric, which is then shrunk. The higher rate of shrinkage for the polyester causes the *washi* thread to undulate within the confines of the outer cloth. In **Feather Flurries** (plate 65), Sudo has inserted feathers by hand into woven, rectangular pockets of silk organdy. The frosted moiré of the organdy gives the feathers a feeling of suspension in air similar to Miyamoto's **Airy Weave** (plate 63) where a free-floating middle layer of electric blue thread moves independently of the two outer layers. Miyamoto accomplishes this by weaving without the warp thread on this middle layer, leaving the weft threads to hang freely.

All of these artists, designers, and manufacturers exemplify a commitment to a long Japanese tradition of combining technology of the hand with the creative spirit of the mind. Each quality is equally valued and aspired to, but it is the assimilation of both that distinguishes the finest work. A direct outgrowth has been the unmediated beauty that each embodies, regardless of function. A fishing net can fulfill aesthetic expectations about trans-

21. Detail of **Composition Ito-Kukan**

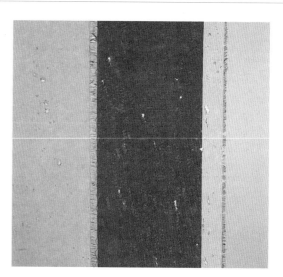

22. Detail of **Grinded Fabric—Ocher: RF#4**

parency as readily as the finest silk weaving, and the ominously rich blue of indigo can be attained through both natural and synthetic means. The organic and inorganic coexist to the extent that they define each other through their opposition. The vocabulary associated with natural beauty— phrases like "glowing sunset," "reflections on the surface of water," or "birch bark"—captures the essential spirit of the work of these artists whether the medium is carbon fiber, polyurethane, or silk. These images are the sources of inspiration for the designers as they create functional fabrics and highly articulated surfaces.

The successful integration of opposing extremes—tradition with technology or practicality with aesthetic—in these textiles results in an extra-ordinary collection of beautiful artifacts. These fabrics perpetuate the modern spirit by maintaining a seamless flow between beauty and function, past and present. The ability to do so insures their time-lessness and value to our visual world.

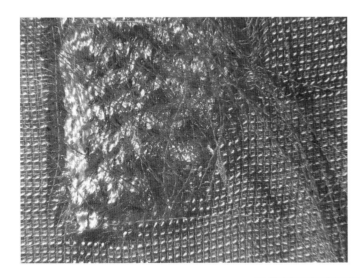

23. Detail of **Moss Temple**

This essay is dedicated to my grand-mother, Anna Lange Bancroft, who first instilled in me a curator's love and respect for textiles.

Notes

1. I would like to thank all of the artists, designers, and manufacturers who have generously explained their work processes to Cara and me. As much as possible, I have used their own words to describe the techniques. In some cases, individuals and factories have divulged their "secret recipes" for the first time, which I know will be an inspiration to anyone interested in textiles.

2. "Kijoka Banana Fiber," *The Traditional Crafts of Japan,* vol. 2, p. 120.

3. Conversation with her daughter-in-law Mieko Taira, May 1997.

4. This and subsequent quotes by the artists are taken from conversations and interviews with the curators from May 1997 to April 1998.

5. A denier is a unit of fineness for yarn. One gram of one denier yarn measures 9 kilometers, or 5.4 miles.

6. These are Indian dyes derived from fruit. For the past ten years, the Makis have made regular visits to northern India to handweave their exquisite shawls and yardage fabrics.

7. Metallic fibers and surfaces have appeared for centuries in Japanese tex-tiles and were used to achieve a luxuri-ous and glimmering surface on *kosode* (literally "small sleeves"), the standard outer robe since the sixteenth century and used for costumes in Noh dramas and kimonos.

8. Yoshiko Wada, Mary Kellogg Rice, Jane Barton, *Shibori: The Inventive Art of Japanese Shaped Resist Dyeing* (New York and Tokyo: Kodansha International, 1983), p. 7.

9. Amanda Mayer Stinchecum, "Kosode: Techniques and Designs," in Stinchecum, *Kosode: 16th–19th Century Textiles from the Nomura Collection* (New York: Japan Society and Kodansha International, 1984), p. 23.

10. This is a handmade paper from the Mino region in central Honshu that is used to make *shoji,* or sliding paper doors, because of its strength.

11. This paste was once used in Japanese paper robe manufacturing and now is used to make paper bags and pouches because of its water-resistant and hardening qualities.

12. Traditionally used for interior wall surfaces in Japanese homes and tea rooms, this soil is named after the area of Kyoto where it can be found.

The plate captions list artist or designer, title of work, date, material, process, dimensions, manufacturer, and, if applicable, collection. The dimension listed indicates the roll width, unless the work is a unique or collection piece, in which case both dimensions (width x length) are given. The location following the manufacturer is the prefecture where the company or factory is found. An asterisk indicates that an example of the fabric is in the collection of both The Museum of Modern Art, New York, and The Saint Louis Art Museum, though the photographed sample is in the collection named. Unless otherwise indicated, all other works were kindly provided by the artist, designer, or manufacturer.

Plates

TRANSPARENT

1. REIKO SUDO

Stratus. 1992
Silk. Plain weave, starch resist dyed,
29 1/2 x 123" (74.9 x 312.4 cm)
Mfr.: Nuno Corporation, Tokyo;
also Maruya Senko Co., Ltd., Kyoto
Collection The Saint Louis Art Museum.*
Gift of Nuno Corporation

2. AKIKO ISHIGAKI

Indigo-Dyed Silk. 1997
Silk. Handwoven twill, dyed with
Ryukyu and Indian indigo,
20" (50.8 cm) wide

3. SAKASE ADTECH CO., LTD.

Triaxial Fabric. 1991
Carbon fiber. Triaxial weave,
62" (157.5 cm) wide
Mfr.: Sakase Adtech Co., Ltd., Fukui

4. REIKO SUDO

Shutter. 1997
Nylon. Stitched on soluble base fabric, base
dissolved, 32 ³/₈" (82.2 cm) wide
Mfr.: Nuno Corporation, Tokyo

5. TORAY INDUSTRIES, INC.

Encircling Fishing Net. 1996
Teteron polyester. Knotless mesh net, variable
width (1 ¹/₂" contracted / 132" expanded) x
278" (3.8/335.3 x 706.1 cm)
Mfr.: Toray Industries Inc., Tokyo;
also Nitto Seimo Co., Ltd., Tokyo
Collection The Museum of Modern Art,
New York. Gift of Toray Industries, Inc.

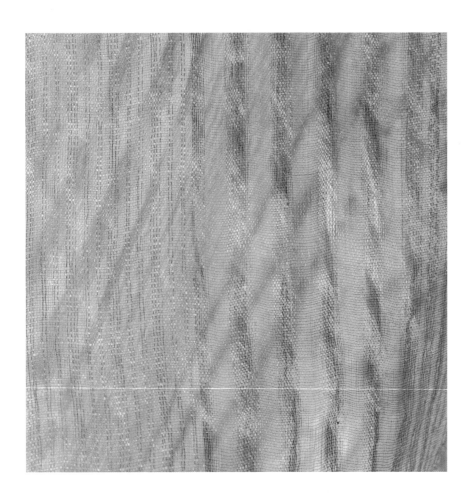

6. MICHIKO UEHARA

Tobi Gasuri (Alternating Kasuri). 1997
Silk. Handwoven, ten-to-twenty-five-denier
yarn, *kasuri* dyed with *fukugi* and *annatto*,
24 x 100" (60.9 x 254 cm)

7. MICHIKO UEHARA

Lower layer:
Yuyake (Evening Glow). 1991
Silk. Handwoven double weave, ten-denier
yarn, dyed with *annatto*, madder, and
gromwell, 20 x 250" (50.8 x 635 cm)

Upper layer:
Sogen (Grassy Plains). 1997
Silk. Handwoven double weave,
ten-to-twenty-seven-denier yarn, dyed with
indigo and *rengyo*, 24 x 100" (60.9 x 254 cm)

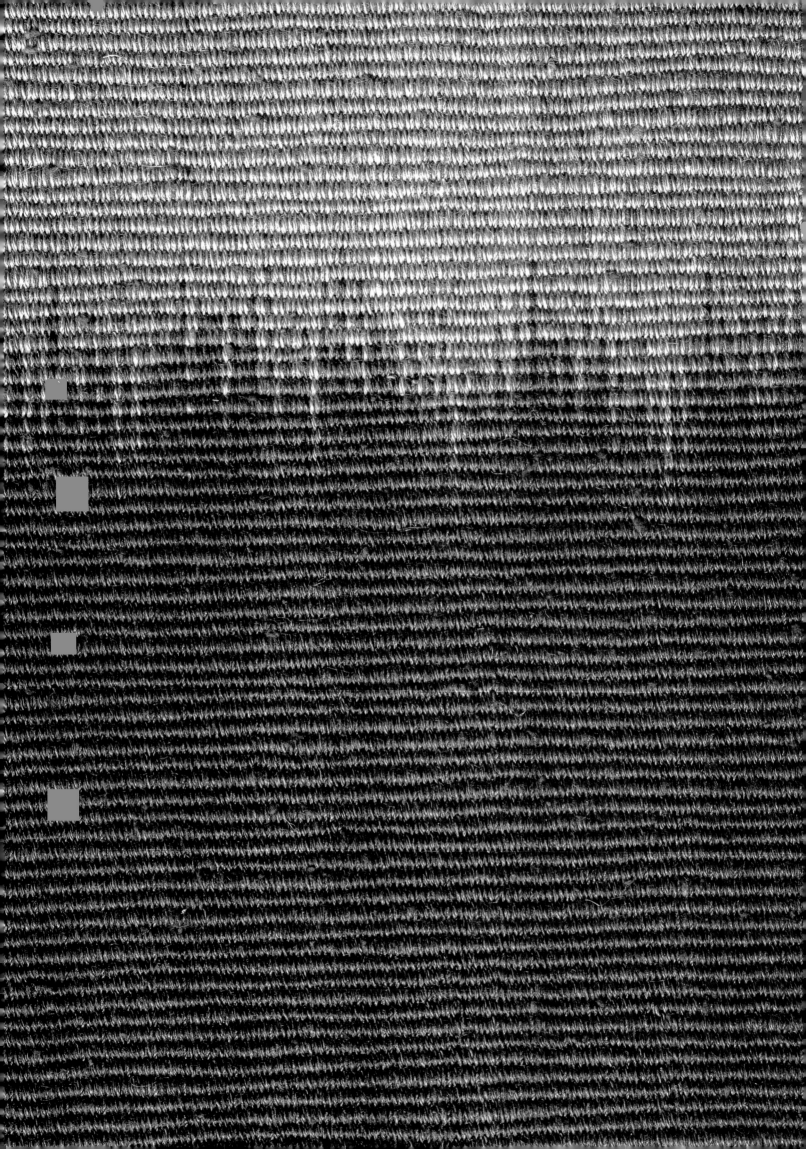

8. JUN TOMITA

Kasuri Panel 151-1 (detail)
(see plate 9)

9. JUN TOMITA

Kasuri Panel 151-1. 1993
Silk, hemp, and linen. Handwoven, *ikat* dyed,
39 ¼ x 80 ¼" (99.7 x 203.9 cm)
Collection Sheila Hicks

10. HIROYUKI SHINDO

Shindigo Square Series 92-1. 1992
Cotton and linen. Handwoven, gradation dyed
with indigo, 76 x 77" (193 x 195.6 cm)
Collection The Saint Louis Art Museum.
Friends Fund

11. HIROYUKI SHINDO

Shindigo Square Series 92-1 (detail)

12. CHIAKI MAKI

Left: **Flux**. 1996
Malda, dupion, and tassar silk.
Handwoven plain and twill weave,
malda silk dyed with indigo and *anar*,
25" (63.5 cm) wide
Mfr.: Maki Textile Studio, Tokyo;
also Tal, New Delhi, India

Right: **Capriccio**. 1996
Wool, malda silk, and tassar silk.
Jacquard weave, malda silk dyed in *harad*,
27" (68.6 cm) wide
Mfr.: Maki Textile Studio, Tokyo;
also Tal, New Delhi, India
Collection Sheila Hicks

13. CHIAKI MAKI

Hollow Bamboo. 1997
Malda and tassar silk. Handwoven plain
weave, dyed with *harad* and *anar*,
27" (68.6 cm) wide
Mfr.: Maki Textile Studio, Tokyo;
also Tal, New Delhi, India

14. BRIDGESTONE METALPHA CORPORATION

Silksteel Sculpture by Sheila Hicks. 1997–98
Alphatex™. Wire drawn and acid-pickled,
14 x 14" (35.6 x 35.6 cm)
Mfr.: Bridgestone Metalpha Corporation,
Tochigi
Collection the manufacturer and the artist

REFLECTIVE

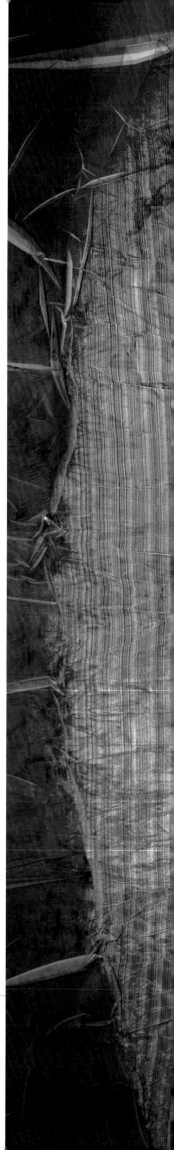

15. JUNICHI ARAI

Moon Light. 1992
Micro-slit polyester film with aluminum,
wool, and nylon filament. "Melt-off" and
shibori dyed, 31 x 130" (78.7 x 330.2 cm)
Mfr.: Kay Tay, Fukui;
also Oike Industrial Co., Ltd., Kyoto
Collection The Saint Louis Art Museum.
Gift of the designer

16. JUNICHI ARAI

Deep Sea. 1994
Polyester and aluminum. "Melt-off" and
heat-transfer printed, 42 x 216"
(106.7 x 548.6 cm)
Mfr.: Kay Tay, Fukui;
also Oike Industrial Co., Ltd., Kyoto
Collection The Saint Louis Art Museum.
Gift of the designer

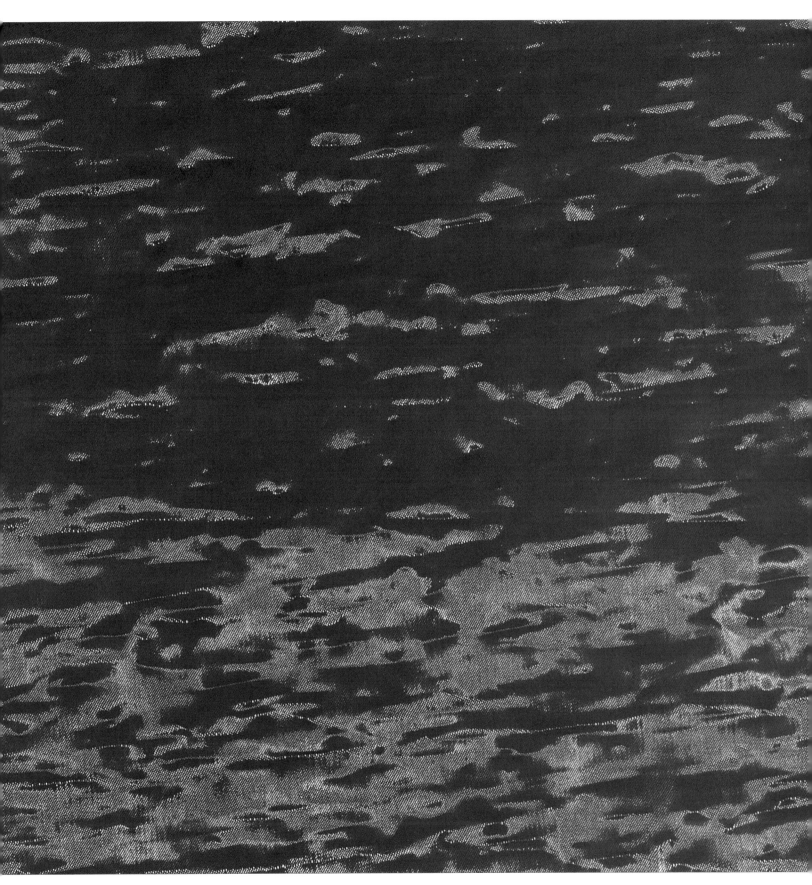

17. KOICHI YOSHIMURA, WITH REIKO SUDO

Blue Mirror Cloth with Wrinkles. 1995
(Cloth without wrinkles originally designed
by Makiko Minagawa with Yoshimura, 1990)
Polyester and polyester monofilament. Satin weave,
43" (109.2 cm) wide
Mfr.: S. Yoshimura Co., Ltd., Fukui;
also Seiren Co., Ltd., Fukui

18. KOICHI YOSHIMURA

Iridescent Satin. 1994
Polyester monofilament and cotton. Satin
weave, piece-dyed, 44" (111.8 cm) wide
Mfr.: S. Yoshimura Co., Ltd., Fukui;
also Senken Co., Ltd., Fukui

19. REIKO SUDO

Stainless Steel Gloss. 1990
Polyester. Plain weave, calender pressed and
"spatter-plated," 44 1/4 x 245" (112.4 x 622.3 cm)
Mfr.: Nuno Corporation, Tokyo;
also Kanebo Spinning Co., Ltd., Osaka
Collection The Museum of Modern Art,
New York.* Gift of Nuno Corporation

20. REIKO SUDO

Copper Cloth. 1993
Copper and Promix™. Single weave,
38 1/2 x 315" (97.8 x 800.1 cm)
Mfr.: Nuno Corporation, Tokyo;
also Tsuguo Co., Ltd., Yamanashi
Collection The Museum of Modern Art,
New York. Gift of Nuno Corporation

PRINTED

21. KEIJI OTANI
Technical process: REIKO SUDO

Brickyard. 1997
Nylon and polyurethane. Screenprinted,
39⅜" (97.5 cm) wide
Mfr.: Nuno Corporation, Tokyo;
also Umetani Craft, Kyoto

22. REIKO SUDO
Transfer print technique: HIROKO SUWA

Scrapyard (Nail). 1994
Rayon with transfer print. Hand printed,
22 x 62 ¼" (55.9 x 158.1 cm)
Mfr.: Nuno Corporation, Tokyo;
also Kanebo Spinning Co., Ltd., Osaka
Collection The Saint Louis Art Museum.
Gift of Nuno Corporation

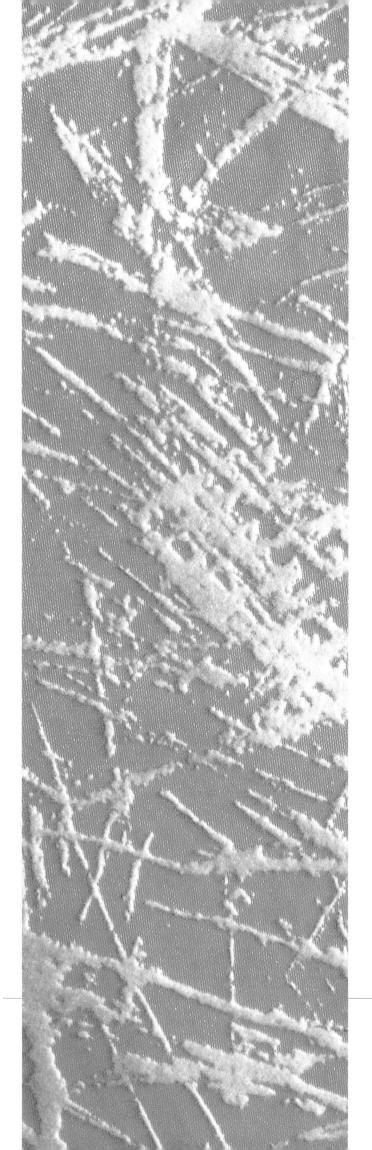

Overleaf

23. REIKO SUDO

Graffiti. 1995
Polyester. Flock printed,
48 x 254" (121.9 x 645.2 cm)
Mfr.: Nuno Corporation, Tokyo;
also Kimura Senko Co., Ltd., Shiga
Collection The Museum of Modern Art,
New York. Gift of Nuno Corporation

24. REIKO SUDO

Scattered Rubber Bands. 1997
Linen, acrylic, and silicone.
Screenprinted, 44 1/16" (111.9 cm) wide
Mfr.: Nuno Corporation, Tokyo;
also Umetani Craft, Kyoto

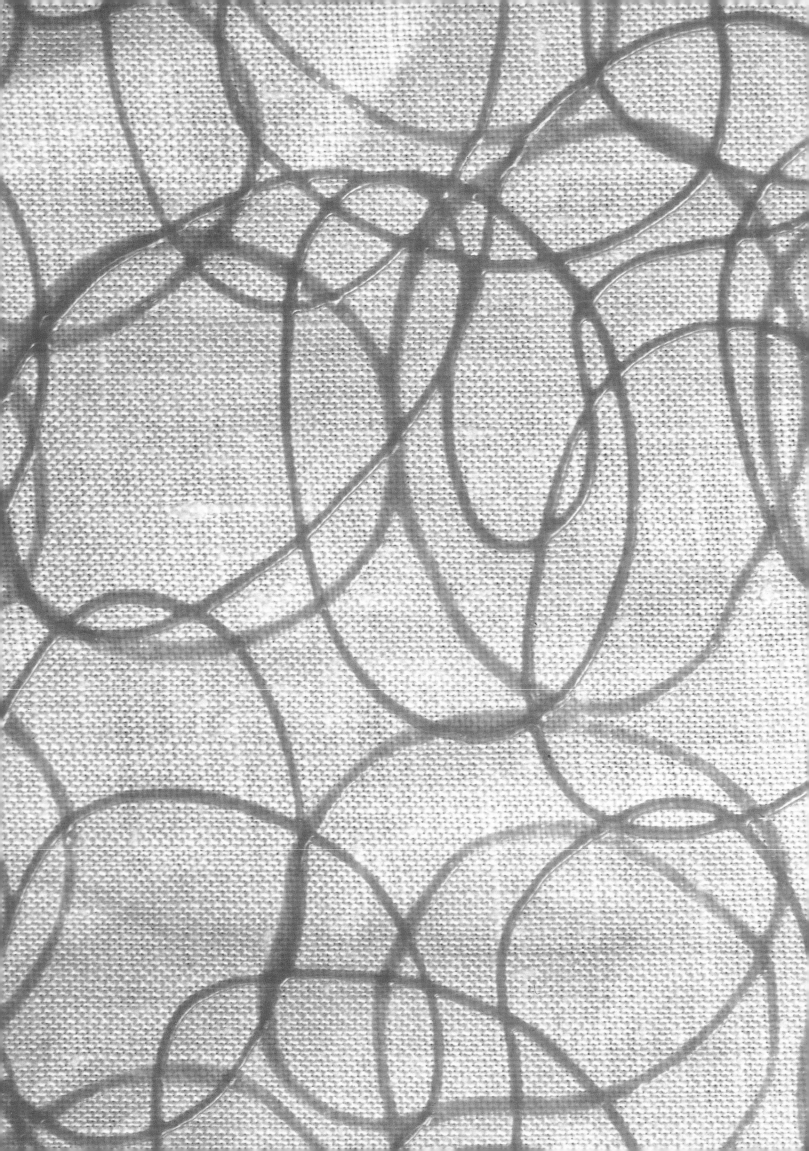

25. YOSHIHIRO KIMURA

Pedocal. 1996
Nylon, polyurethane, polyester, and rayon.
Flock printed, 44" (111.8 cm) wide
Mfr.: Kimura Senko Co., Ltd., Shiga

28. JÜRGEN LEHL

Foreground:
Shawl. 1995
Silk. Pleated, stitched, steamed, handpainted,
and discharge dyed, 15³/₄ x 70⁷/₈"
(40.0 x 180 cm)
Mfr.: Jürgen Lehl, Tokyo

Background:
Shawl. 1997
Silk. Pleated, stitched, and gradation dyed,
23⁵/₈ x 70⁷/₈" (59.9 x 180 cm)
Mfr.: Jürgen Lehl, Tokyo

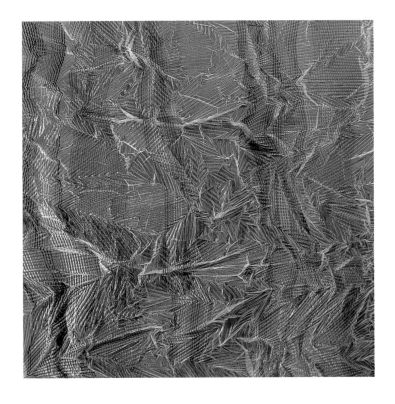

26. JUNICHI ARAI

Charred Fabric. 1991
Micro-slit nylon film with aluminum, wool,
and nylon filament. "Melt-off," *shibori* dyed,
and felted, 25" (63.5 cm) wide
Mfr.: Kay Tay, Fukui;
also Oike Industrial Co., Ltd., Kyoto

27. JUNICHI ARAI

Yuragi (Fluctuation). Designed 1985,
manufactured 1994
Polyester and nylon. "Melt-off" and pleated,
32 x 240" (81.3 x 609.6 cm)
Mfr.: Daito Pleats Co. Ltd., Gumma;
also Oike Industrial Co., Ltd., Kyoto
Collection The Museum of Modern Art, New York.
Gift of the designer

28. JÜRGEN LEHL

Foreground:
Shawl. 1995
Silk. Pleated, stitched, steamed, handpainted, and discharge dyed, 15 3/4 x 70 7/8"
(40.0 x 180 cm)
Mfr.: Jürgen Lehl, Tokyo

Background:
Shawl. 1997
Silk. Pleated, stitched, and gradation dyed, 23 5/8 x 70 7/8" (59.9 x 180 cm)
Mfr.: Jürgen Lehl, Tokyo

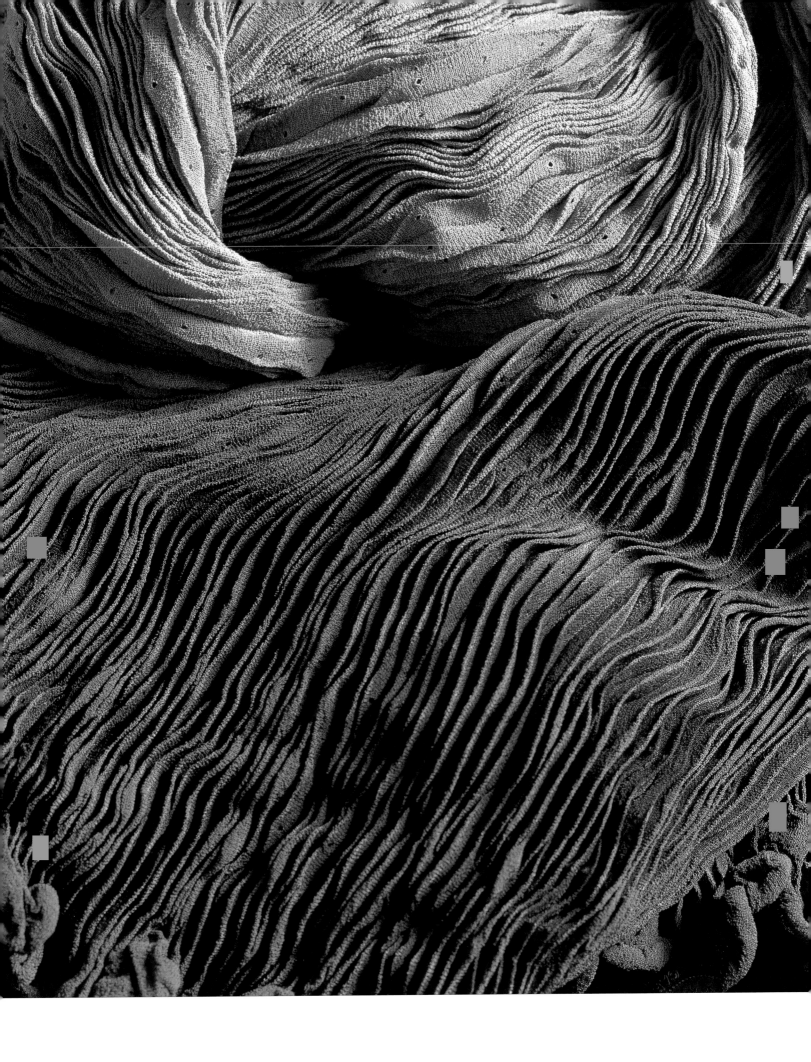

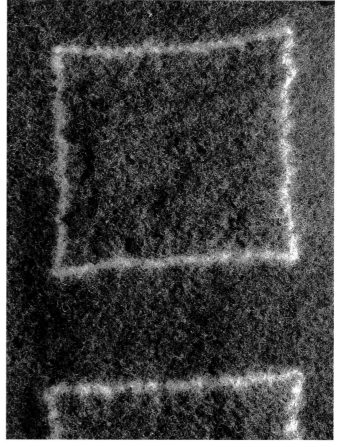

29. OSAMU MITA

Wool Mesh Window. 1997
Wool. Double layer plain weave, cut and felted,
33" (83.8 cm) wide
Mfr.: Mitasho Co., Ltd., Gumma

30. OSAMU MITA

Wool Mesh Window (reverse)

31. OSAMU MITA

Washi & Wool. 1997
Wool and *washi* paper. Jacquard double
weave: plain weave (*washi* paper), mesh
weave (wool), felted, 25" (63.5 cm) wide
Mfr.: Mitasho Co., Ltd., Gumma

32. OSAMU MITA

Washi & Wool (reverse)

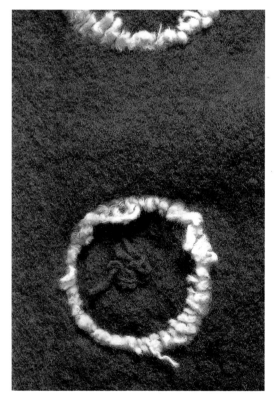

33. HIDEKO TAKAHASHI

Stick. 1996
Wool and tulle. Jacquard double weave,
felted, rolled, and dyed, 37" (93.9 cm) wide
Mfr.: Mitasho Co., Ltd., Gumma; also Textile
Research Institute of Gumma, Gumma

34. HIDEKO TAKAHASHI

Circle Square II. 1995
Wool. Jacquard triple weave, cut, felted,
and dyed, 18" (45.7 cm) wide
Mfr.: Mitasho Co., Ltd., Gumma; also Textile
Research Institute of Gumma, Gumma

35. HIDEKO TAKAHASHI

Circle Square II (reverse)

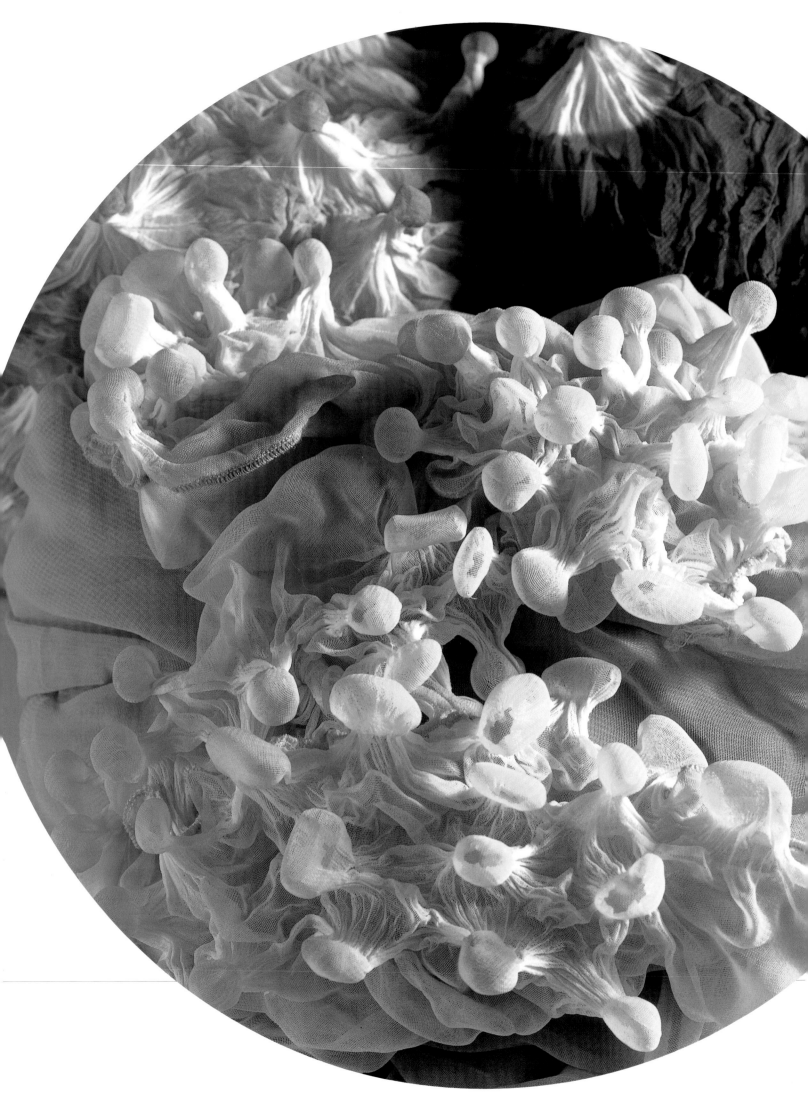

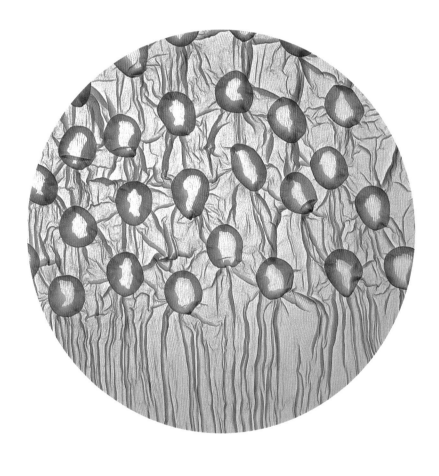

36. YUH OKANO

Epidermis (Ocean). 1994
Polyester. *Shibori* dyed and heat set,
each 25" (63.5 cm) wide
Mfr.: Daito Pleats Co., Ltd., Gumma

37. YUH OKANO

Epidermis (Forest). 1997
Polyester. *Shibori* dyed and heat pressed,
30" (76.2 cm) wide
Mfr.: Daito Pleats Co., Ltd., Gumma

38. INOUE PLEATS CO., LTD.

Accordion Wrinkle. 1996
Polyester. Hand pleated and heat set,
47" (119.4 cm) wide
Mfr.: Inoue Pleats Co., Ltd., Fukui

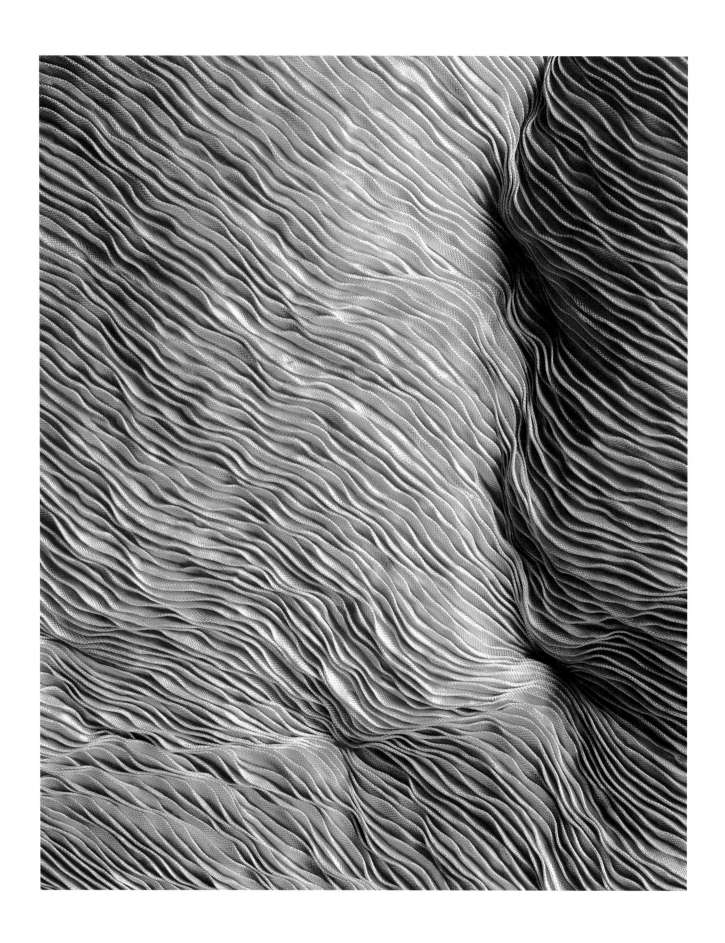

39. INOUE PLEATS CO., LTD.

Crystal Σ. 1997
Polyester. Machine pleated and manually
compressed, 59" (149.9 cm) wide
Mfr.: Inoue Pleats Co., Ltd., Fukui

40. INOUE PLEATS CO., LTD.

Wrinkle P. 1995
Polyester. Hand pleated and heat set,
59" (149.9 cm) wide
Mfr.: Inoue Pleats Co., Ltd., Fukui

41. INOUE PLEATS CO., LTD.

Majolica. 1996
Polyester. Machine parallel pleated
[weft before warp], 59" (149.9 cm) wide
Mfr.: Inoue Pleats Co., Ltd., Fukui

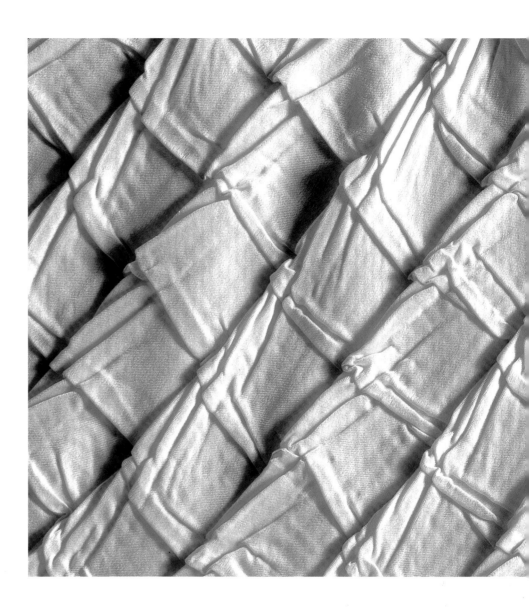

Overleaf

42. INOUE PLEATS CO., LTD.

Square L. 1996
Polyester. Machine side pleated
[weft before warp], 59" (149.9 cm) wide
Mfr.: Inoue Pleats Co., Ltd., Fukui

43. INOUE PLEATS CO., LTD.

Blizzard. 1996
Polyester. Machine side pleated,
59" (149.9 cm) wide
Mfr.: Inoue Pleats Co., Ltd., Fukui

44. REIKO SUDO
Pleating technique: HIROAKI TAKEKURA

Mica. 1995
Polyester. Heat molded, machine and manually
pleated, 33 x 234 1/4" (83.8 x 595 cm)
Mfr.: Nuno Corporation, Tokyo;
also Takekura Co., Ltd., Gumma
Collection The Museum of Modern Art,
New York. Gift of Nuno Corporation

45. REIKO SUDO
Pleating technique: MIZUE OKADA

Origami Pleat Scarf. 1997
Polyester. Hand pleated and heat-transfer
printed, 17 5/16 x 59 1/16" (43.9 x 150 cm)
Mfr.: Nuno Corporation, Tokyo;
also Takekura Co., Ltd., Gumma

46. REIKO SUDO

Jellyfish. 1993
Polyester. Screenprinted and flash heated,
34 x 251" (86.4 x 637.5 cm)
Mfr.: Nuno Corporation, Tokyo;
also Kimura Senko Co., Ltd., Shiga
Collection The Museum of Modern Art,
New York. Gift of Nuno Corporation

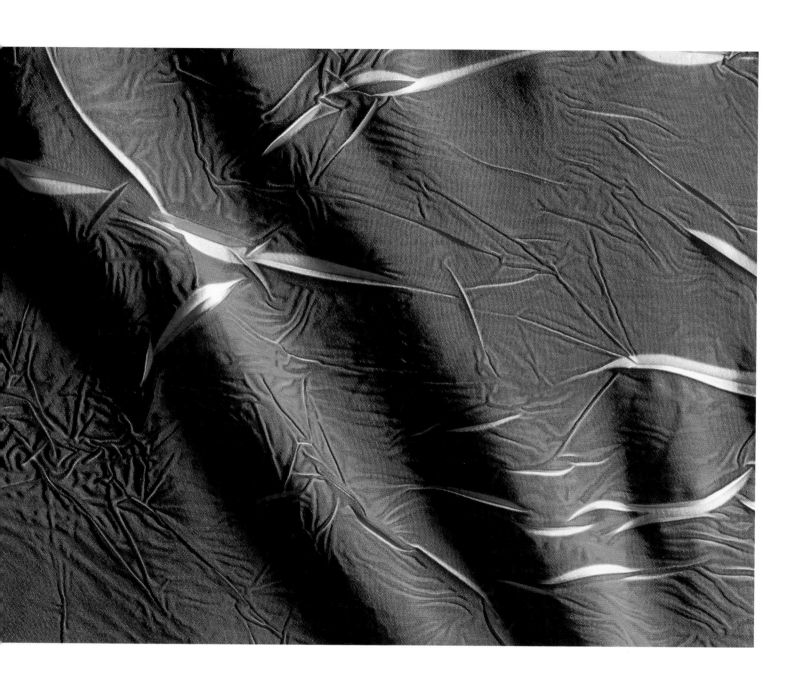

47. URASE CO., LTD.

Harmony. 1997
Polyester. Heat-transfer printed,
40" (101.6 cm) wide
Mfr.: Urase Co., Ltd., Fukui

48. MASAJI YAMAZAKI

Wave Process Velvet. 1993
Polyester and rayon. Screenprinted and flash
heated, 23 x 190" (58.4 x 482.6 cm)
Mfr.: Yamazaki Vellodo Co., Ltd., Fukui;
also Kimura Senko Co., Ltd., Shiga
Collection The Museum of Modern Art,
New York. Gift of Yamazaki Vellodo Co., Ltd.

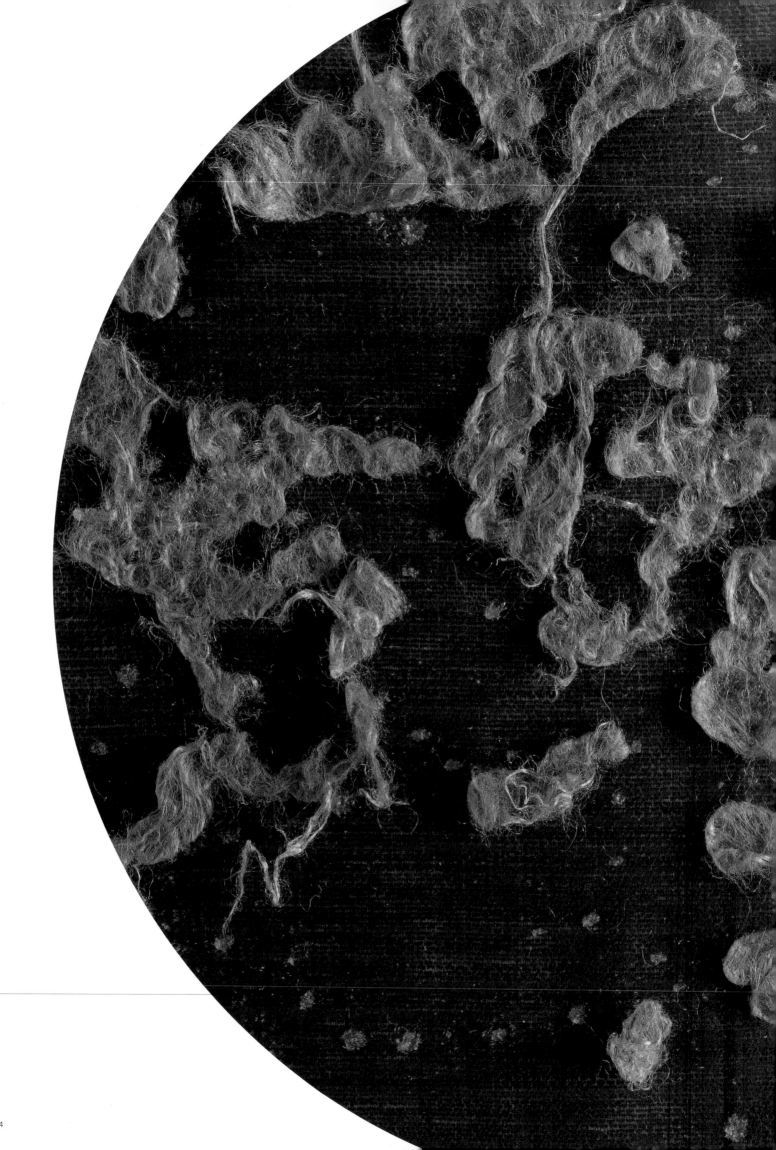

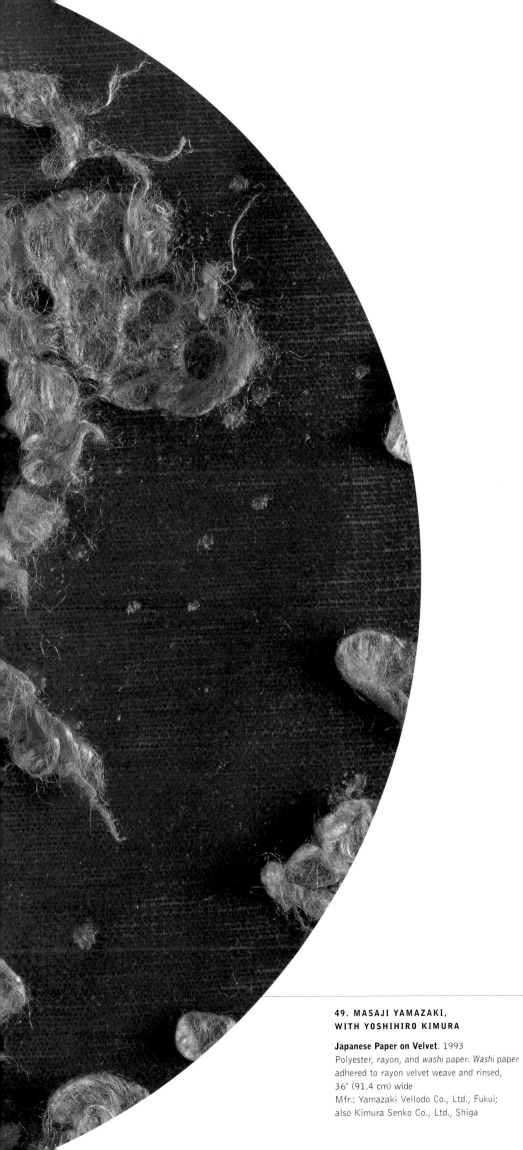

**49. MASAJI YAMAZAKI,
WITH YOSHIHIRO KIMURA**

Japanese Paper on Velvet. 1993
Polyester, rayon, and *washi* paper. *Washi* paper
adhered to rayon velvet weave and rinsed,
36" (91.4 cm) wide
Mfr.: Yamazaki Vellodo Co., Ltd., Fukui;
also Kimura Senko Co., Ltd., Shiga

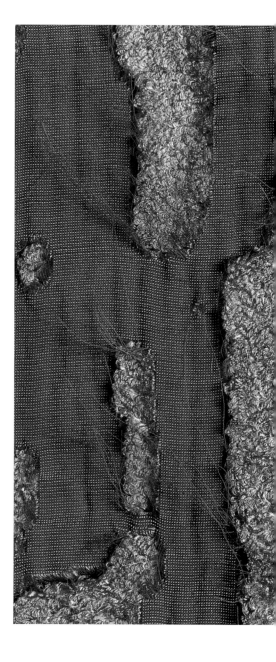

50. REIKO SUDO

Crackle Cloth. 1992
Polyester and rayon. Screenprinted and
chemically etched, 46 x 177" (111.8 x 449.6 cm)
Mfr.: Nuno Corporation, Tokyo;
also Kimura Senko Co., Ltd., Shiga
Collection The Museum of Modern Art,
New York. Gift of Nuno Corporation

51. REIKO SUDO

Moss Temple. 1997
Rayon and polyester. Velvet weave,
screenprinted with chemical pigment,
38³/₁₆" (96.9 cm) wide
Mfr.: Nuno Corporation, Tokyo;
also Yamazaki Vellodo Co., Ltd.,
Fukui, and Urase Co., Ltd., Fukui

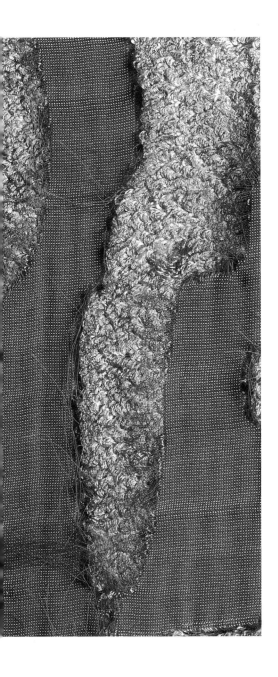

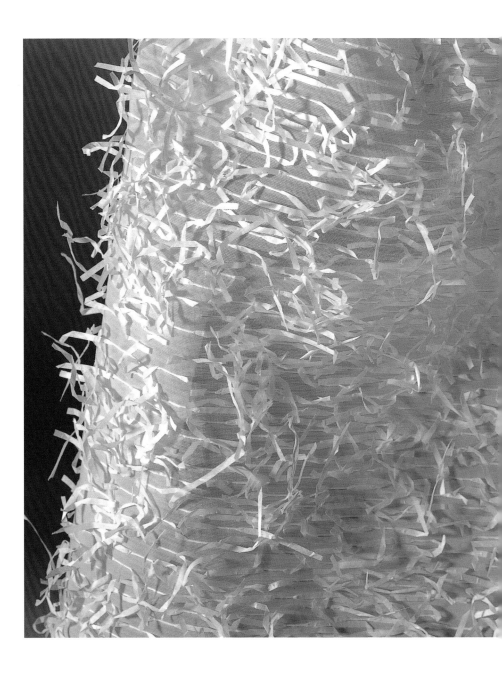

52. REIKO SUDO

Patched Paper. 1997
Polyester and *Mino washi* paper.
Jacquard weave, 44 1/16" (111.9 cm) wide
Mfr.: Nuno Corporation, Tokyo;
also Tsuguo Co., Ltd., Yamanashi

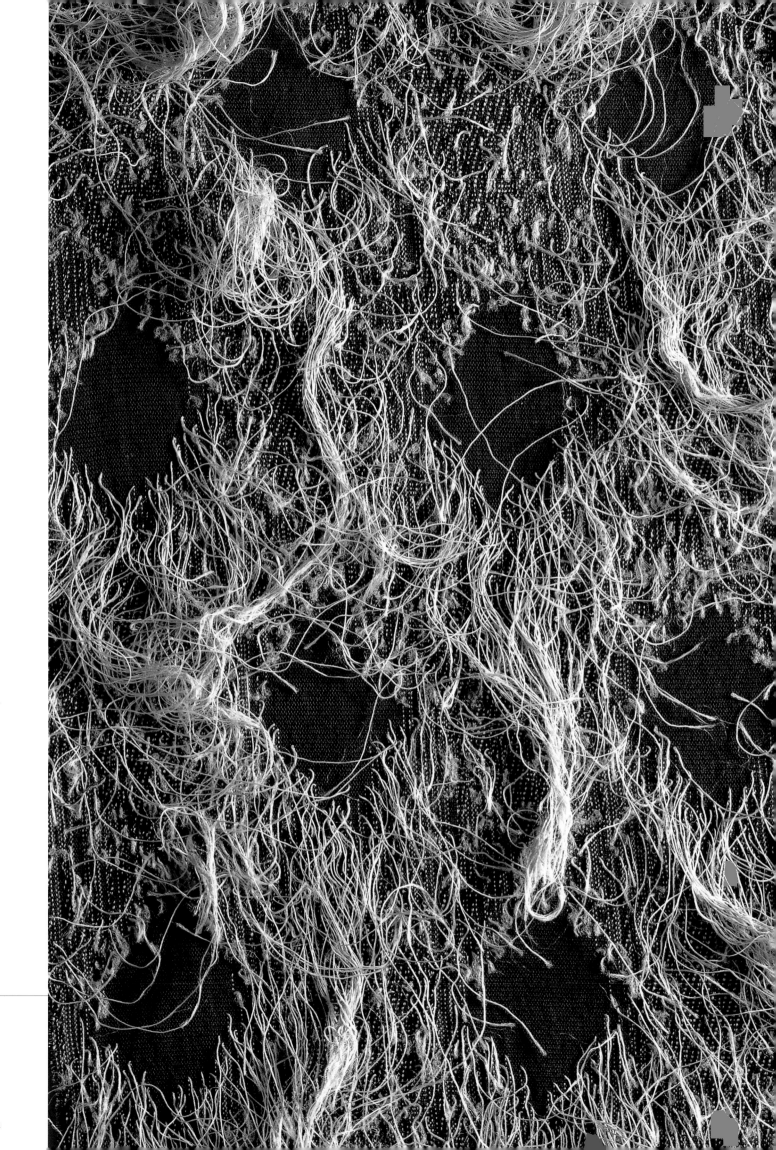

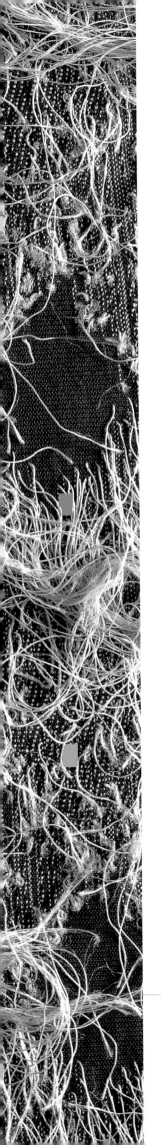
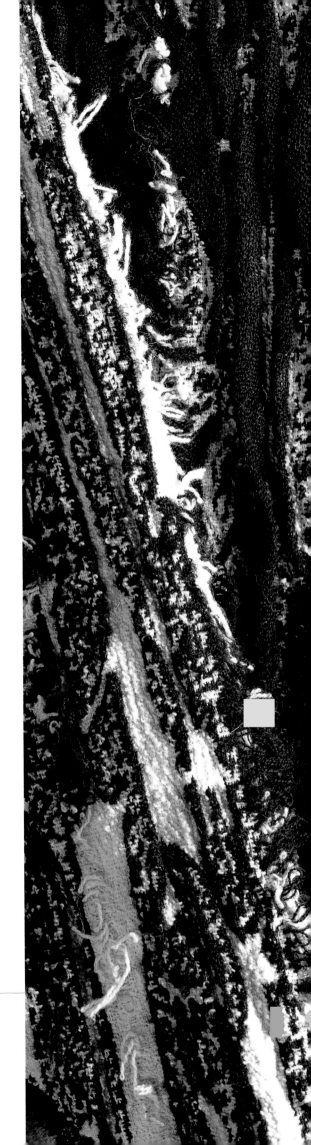

53. AKIHIRO KANEKO

#1926 Brown Hair. 1995
Acetate, rayon, and cupra.
Jacquard weave, cut and dyed,
44" (111.8 cm) wide
Mfr.: Kaneko Orimono Co., Ltd.,
Gumma

54. JUNICHI ARAI

Bark. 1984
Cotton, wool, and polyurethane.
Jacquard double-faced weave,
31" (78.7 cm) wide
Mfr.: Anthologie Co., Ltd., Gumma;
also Hyodo Orimono Co., Ltd., Gumma

55. CHIYOKO TANAKA

Grinded Fabric—Ocher: RF#4. 1986–87
Ramie, linen, and *Jurakudai* soil.
Handwoven, rubbed and polished,
39 3/8 x 97 1/4 " (100 x 247 cm)
Collection The Saint Louis Art Museum.
Friends Fund

56. CHIYOKO TANAKA

Grinded Fabric—Ocher: RF#4 (detail)

57. ISSEY MIYAKE

Runway photograph of Prism Series. 1997

58. ISSEY MIYAKE
Textile Director: MAKIKO MINAGAWA

Prism Series: Coat. 1997
Wool, polyester chiffon, and batting.
Polyester chiffon and batting hand applied
and needlepunched
Mfr.: Issey Miyake Inc., Tokyo

59. ISSEY MIYAKE
Textile Director: MAKIKO MINAGAWA

Prism Series: Coat (detail)

60. ISSEY MIYAKE

Runway photograph of Prism Series. 1997

61. ISSEY MIYAKE

Runway photograph of Star Burst Series. 1998

62. ISSEY MIYAKE
Textile Director: MAKIKO MINAGAWA

Star Burst Series:
Long Shirt and Pants (detail). 1998
Cotton, silver foil, and copper foil.
Woven and heat pressed
Mfr.: Issey Miyake Inc., Tokyo

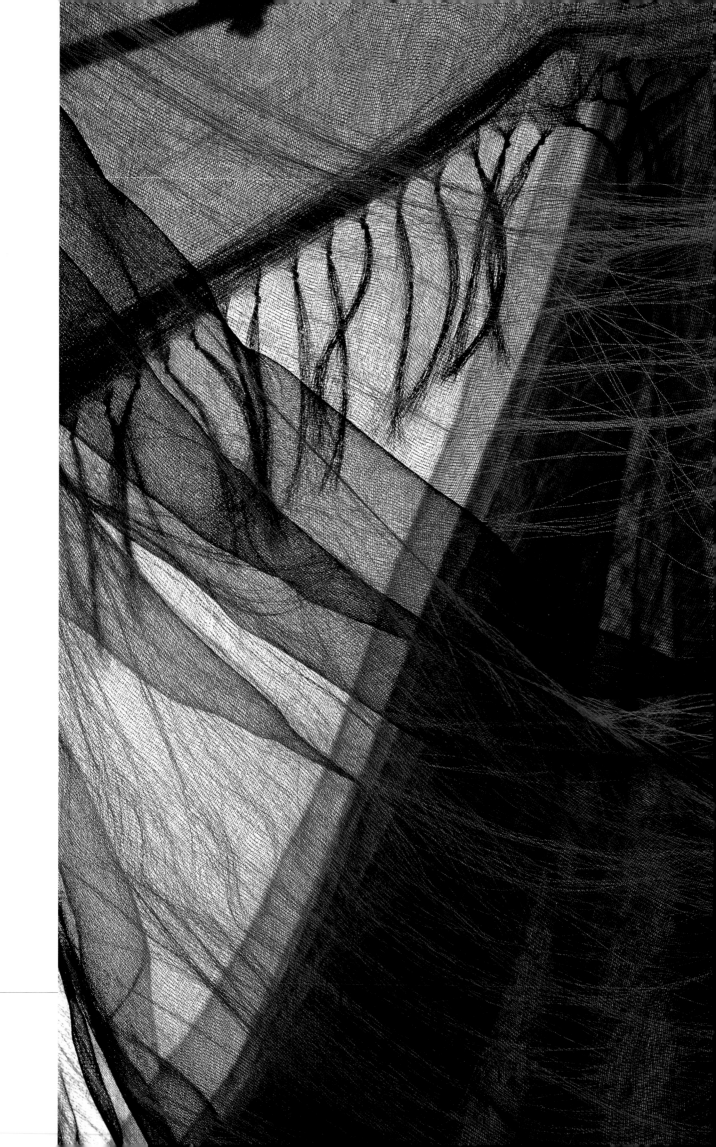

Overleaf

63. EIJI MIYAMOTO

Airy Weave. 1995
Silk. Triple weave, 33 1/2 x 77"
(85.1 x 195.6 cm)
Mfr.: Miyashin Co., Ltd., Tokyo
Collection The Museum of Modern
Art, New York. Gift of the designer

64. NAOMI KOBAYASHI

Composition Ito-Kukan. 1992
Washi paper, *koyori* thread, and *konnyaku*
paste. Hand formed and pasted,
28 x 74" (71.1 x 187.9 cm)
Collection Sheila Hicks

65. REIKO SUDO

Feather Flurries. 1993
Silk organdy and feathers. Double weave,
46 x 78" (116.8 x 158.1 cm)
Mfr.: Nuno Corporation, Tokyo;
also Tsuguo Co., Ltd., Yamanashi
Collection The Museum of Modern Art,
New York.* Gift of Nuno Corporation

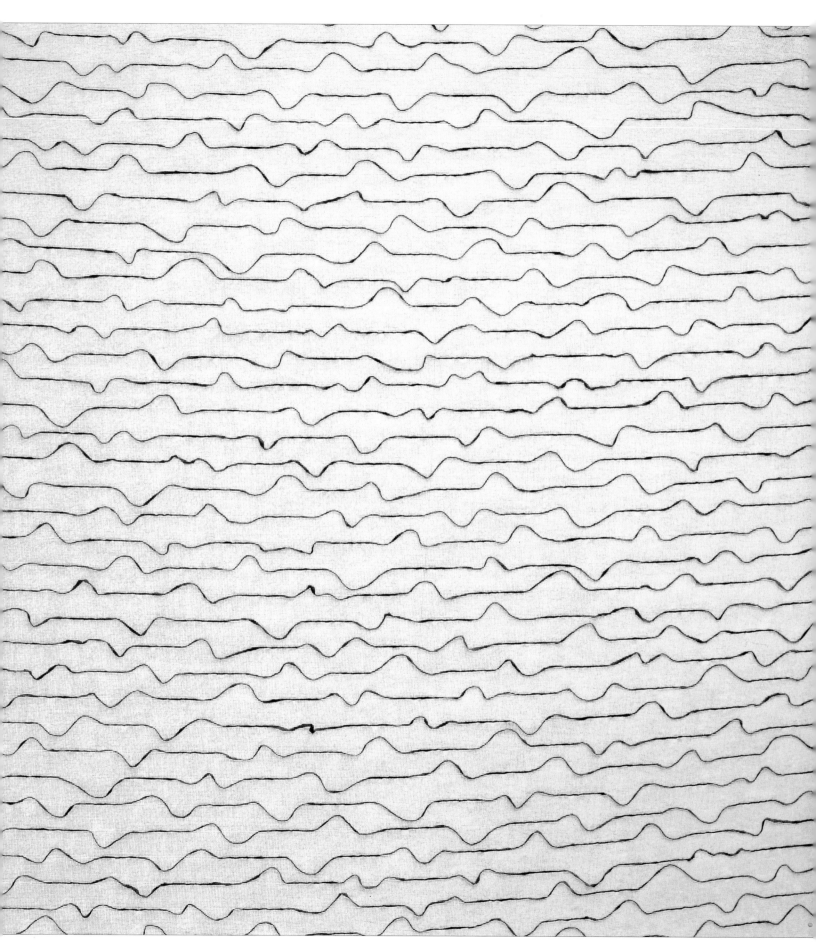

66. AKIHIRO KANEKO

#2765 Yuragi (Fluctuation). 1997
Polyester and *washi* paper. Jacquard double
weave, shrunk, 41" (104.1 cm) wide
Mfr.: Kaneko Orimono Co., Ltd., Gumma

Glossary

ai: natural indigo

aishi: indigo growers

asa: a general term for a variety of bast fibers or woody plant fibers, used specifically to denote hemp. S

basho: a type of banana plant particular to the making of cloth

basho-fu: cloth made from the basho plant

batting: a fibrous material sold in sheets or rolls used for warm interlining or as a type of stuffing for quilts. ET

binder: an adhesive material, a cementing substance

burn-out: a technique developed by Junichi Arai in which the cotton surface of metallic thread is dissolved exposing the metallic core. The inversion of melt-off. H

calender: a machine in which cloth, paper, etc., is pressed by rollers to provide glaze, glossiness, hardness, luster, sheen, and even embossed designs. ET/OED

choma: China grass

denier: originally, a coin used as a unit to measure the weight of silk, equal to 1/24 ounce (1.181 grams); now, a unit of fineness of yarn equal to the weight in grams of nine kilometers of it. ET/OED

doncho: a stage curtain

felting: a heat and mechanical process to give woven cloth a thick, compact substantial feel, finish, and appearance. The construction of the cloth is usually concealed after it has undergone this technique. ET/OED

floating weft/warp: the portion of a warp or weft yarn that extends over two or more adjacent weft threads or warp ends in weaving for the purpose of forming certain designs. ET

flock printing: after screenprinting a fabric or other material with an adhesive, rayon fiber measuring 0.5–1 millimeter is either sprayed on top of the material using compressed air, or the fibers are raised vertically using an electrostatic method. This process gives the material an effect of plush suede or velvet. ET

gumbo: the combination of other materials such as silk or ramie in the weaving process

harness: the frame upon which the guide cords used in weaving cloth are placed. ET

heat transfer: a transfer of designs and colors onto the surface of fabrics using heat. H

ikat: the process of patterning cloth by binding yarns before weaving in order to protect areas from dye; it requires careful calculation of where the protected areas of yarn will appear in the final woven piece. S

jacquard: designates an attachment to a loom which enables an intricate pattern in the cloth to be produced automatically by means of punched cards. OED

kasuri: the Japanese term for ikat. S

katazome: a paste-resist stencil dyeing technique. B

konnyaku: a type of paste

melt-off: a technique developed by Junichi Arai in which the metallic fiber in a slit film is dissolved leaving behind a transparent cloth. The inversion of burn-out. H

mengikat: a Malay-Indonesian word meaning "to dye" or "to bind"

needlepunching: a fabric forming method which is widely used in carpets where needles punch through a web of fibers thereby entangling them. ET

okkochi: "the eastern wind" or "to let fall"; a dyeing technique

piling: the cut or uncut loops which make the surface of a pile fabric. Common pile cloths include velvet, corduroy, terry cloth, and carpets. ET

ra: an ancient variation of the triaxial weaving structure

resist dye: a form of dyeing in which some of the fabric yarns are chemically treated in the dye bath so that when the fabric has been woven and piece-dyed, they "resist" the action of subsequent coloration. ET

sabi: rust

satin-backing: a process resulting in a two-faced fabric in which one side is dull-finished and the other is a lustrous satin weave. ET

shibori: the process of manipulating and securing particular areas of fabric before dyeing

slit film: a type of thread made by applying vacuum deposit of aluminum onto material which is then coated with lacquer and slit into thin strips

spatter-plated: a technique used to plate or coat a material by uniformly splashing the surface with metal

sukumo: dried indigo leaves

tatami: straw floor mats measuring 85 x 170 centimeters for residences and 95.5 x 191 centimeters for temples and palaces

textile: from the Latin word textilis (from texere, meaning to weave); a woven fabric. Also, any kind of cloth of various materials, such as bonded fabric, that does not require weaving. ET/OED

thermoplastic: refers to types of substances that have the property of softening at higher temperatures, specifically applied to true synthetic fibers. ET

tow: a continuous loose rope of man-made filaments drawn together without twisting. ET

triaxial: a type of weave or fabric that is formed by three interlacing yarns that meet at 60–70 degree angles. The weaving pattern consists of two warp yarns and one weft yarn interwoven at equal angles to form a textile with performance features that exceed traditionally woven materials; having or pertaining to three axes. ET/OED

tsutsu-gaki: a paste-resist dyeing technique using a tube to draw over sketched lines on the fabric. B

urea resin: a type of resin that can withstand very high temperatures

wa: a yarn made from a specific type of washi paper composed of different fibrous plants

warp: the yarns that run lengthwise in a woven fabric. ET

washi: Japanese handmade paper

weft: the threads woven at right angles across a warp in making fabric. OED

Sources:

B: *Beyond the Tanabata Bridge: Traditional Japanese Textiles.* Edited by William Jay Rathbun. Seattle: Thames and Hudson, in association with Seattle Art Museum, 1993.

ET: *Encyclopedia of Textiles.* By the editors of *American Fabrics and Fashion Magazine.* Englewood Cliffs, New Jersey: Prentice-Hall, Inc., 1980.

H: *Hand and Technology. Textile by Junichi Arai '92.* Tokyo: Asahi Shimbun, 1992.

OED: *The New Shorter Oxford English Dictionary.* Oxford and New York: Oxford University Press, 1995.

S: *Shibori: The Inventive Art of Japanese Shaped Resist Dyeing.* Yoshiko Wada, Mary Kellogg Rice, Jane Barton. New York and Tokyo: Kodansha International, 1983.

Biographies

Junichi Arai, born 1932, Gumma
Since 1950 Arai has been working in some aspect of the textile industry, developing new manufacturing processes. In 1984 he co-founded Nuno Corporation, a company and retail store that produces and sells innovative functional fabrics. He has taught textile workshops all over the world, and his works are included in the collections of major museums. He currently teaches at Otsuka Textile Design Institute.

Bridgestone Metalpha Corporation, established 1970, Tochigi
Originally a joint venture with Bridgestone Tire and N.V. Bekaert S.A., in 1969, it became a separate company in 1994. Their material Alphatex™, introduced in 1996, has been included in exhibitions and fashion shows and been the medium for artworks by Junichi Arai, Peter Collingwood, and Sheila Hicks.

Sheila Hicks, born 1934, Hastings, Nebraska. Lives in Paris since 1964
Education: Yale University
In addition to the United States and Europe, Hicks has designed and made textiles in India, Morocco, Chile, and has worked in Saudi Arabia and South Africa. Since 1989 she has realized a number of large-scale textile art commissions in Japan, and in 1996 she became a consultant for a new stainless-steel fiber development at Bridgestone Metalpha Corporation.

Inoue Pleats Company, Ltd., established 1953, Fukui
Initially a trading company, Inoue Pleats began pleats development in 1943. Since the emergence of acetate materials in 1953, their pleats process using thermoplasticity has been in operation. They have a retail store, Pleeets, in Tokyo.

Akiko Ishigaki, born 1938, Okinawa
Education: Women's Junior College of Fine Arts, Tokyo
Ishigaki studied traditional Okinawan dyeing and weaving with Fukumi Shimura, a "Living National Treasure" in 1970 and has been continually researching Okinawan plants for dyestuff. In 1997 she made costumes for the touring performance *Yaeyama Traditional Dance and Textiles.*

Akihiro Kaneko, born 1961, Gumma
Education: Rhode Island School of Design
Kaneko, in addition to designing for his family's mill, Kaneko Orimono, has participated in several textile competitions and group exhibitions in Japan in the last several years. He works often with other designers such as Junichi Arai and Hideko Takahashi.

Yoshihiro Kimura, born 1947, Kyoto
Education: Toyama University
After graduating Kimura worked in his father's textile business which would later specialize in flock printing. They have diversified to include other printing techniques using resin and pigment. He has worked with such well-known designers as Kansai Yamamoto and Issey Miyake.

Naomi Kobayashi, born 1945, Tokyo
Education: Musashino Art University, Tokyo
Since 1969 she has participated in many solo and group exhibitions all over the world including the International Biennale of Tapestry in Lausanne, Switzerland. A major figure in textile arts, her work is included in such collections as The Metropolitan Museum of Art, Cleveland Museum of Art, and The Victoria & Albert Museum, London.

Jürgen Lehl, born 1944, Poland. Lives in Japan since 1971
After working in France between 1962 and 1967, he moved to Japan and founded Jürgen Lehl Co., in 1972. This company designs and sells women's and men's clothing, accessories, and jewelry. He has participated in numerous solo and group exhibitions, most recently in 1997, at the Museum für Angewandte Kunst, in Cologne, Germany.

Chiaki Maki, born 1960, Toyama
Education: Musashino Art University, Tokyo; Rhode Island School of Design
Chiaki has been working with Indian weavers in New Delhi since 1989. She established Maki Textile Studio in 1990 and opened a retail store in 1996 in Tokyo. Her work has been included in exhibitions in Israel, Japan, and India.

Kaori Maki, born 1962, Toyama
Education: Rhode Island School of Design
Kaori worked for Jack Lenor Larsen in 1988 and later with other textile manufacturers before joining Maki Textile Studio in 1992. Her work has been exhibited in galleries in Japan and Germany.

Makiko Minagawa, born Kyoto
Education: Kyoto City University of Art
She was an independent designer before joining Miyake Design Studio in 1971, where she has worked ever since as its textile director. In 1989, *Texture*, a compilation of her work over a seventeen-year period was published by Kodansha. She has been distinguished in the last few years with many fashion and design awards and an exhibition of her work.

Osamu Mita, born 1963, Gumma
Education: Kokugakuin University
He is the third-generation textile producer at Mitasho, which produces women's apparel fabrics. He has worked at Yohji Yamamoto's studio and continues to work with Yamamoto and other designers.

Issey Miyake, born 1938, Hiroshima
Education: Tama Art University
Since presenting his first collection in 1963, Miyake has been one of the most influential voices of fashion. He established Miyake Design Studio in 1970 after studying in Paris and New York. In 1973 he presented his collections in Paris for the first time and continues to show there biannually. His work has been featured in many exhibitions and included in major museum collections all over the world.

Eiji Miyamoto, born 1948, Tokyo
Education: Hosei University
Since joining his father's company in 1975, Miyamoto has been working independently and with renown designers such as Issey Miyake. He has participated in several solo and group exhibitions including *Japanese Design: A Survey Since 1950* at the Philadelphia Museum of Art in 1994.

Yuh Okano, born 1965
Education: Rhode Island School of Design
She has participated in solo and group exhibitions and participated in the International Shibori Conference in India in 1997. She is currently an instructor of textile fiber technique at the Otsuka Textile Design Institute.

Keiji Otani, born 1967, Hyogo
Education: Royal College of Art; Goldsmiths' College, University of London
In 1995–96 Otani worked with designer Jack Lenor Larsen and is currently a clothing and textile designer for Nuno Corporation.

Sakase Adtech Co., Ltd., established 1988, Fukui
Since its founding by the Sakai brothers, Ryoji and Yoshiharu, Sakase has been researching and selling new materials. Their clients are found all over the world and range from aerospace industries to sporting goods manufacturers.

Hiroyuki Shindo, born 1941, Tokyo
Education: Kyoto City University of Art
Shindo's work has been included in many exhibitions worldwide during the past twenty years, most recently in France, India, and Israel. Major museums such as the Stedelijk Museum, Amsterdam; The Art Institute of Chicago; Cleveland Museum of Art; and the Israel Museum, Jerusalem, have collected his work. Since 1997 he has been a professor in and head of the textile department at the Kyoto College of Art.

Reiko Sudo, born 1953, Ibaragi
Education: Musashino Art University, Tokyo
In 1984, Sudo was one of the founders of Nuno Corporation, a company and retail store that produces and sells innovative functional fabrics. Her work has been shown worldwide, included in exhibitions in the United States, India, and Israel. Her work is in collections of the Museum of Fine Arts in Boston; The Victoria & Albert Museum, London; the Philadelphia Museum of Art; and the Cooper-Hewitt National Design Museum in New York.

Toshiko Taira, born 1921, Okinawa
Taira was taught the traditional *basho-fu* technique by her mother Rana Taira. She studied general weaving under Kichinusuke Tonomura in Kurashiki, Okayama Prefecture. She opened her *basho-fu* workshop in 1948 and since then has had exhibitions in Japan, Hawaii, and Washington.

Hideko Takahashi, born 1950, Tokyo
Education: Otsuka Textile Design Institute
She has had several solo exhibitions in Japan and Australia, and her work is included in the Powerhouse Museum in Australia. Since 1988 she has also been a part-time lecturer at the Otsuka Textile Design Institute.

Chiyoko Tanaka, born 1941, Tokyo
Education: Kyoto City University of Art
Tanaka has participated in many exhibitions all over the world, and her work is included in collections such as The Art Institute of Chicago and the Stedelijk Museum, Amsterdam.

Jun Tomita, born 1951, Toyama
Education: The West Surrey College of Art and Design
He has participated in exhibitions all over the world and is included in collections such as the Stedelijk Museum, Amsterdam; The Victoria & Albert Museum, London; and the Denver Art Museum. He has taught at the Kyoto

College of Art, and his work is on permanent display at the renown Tawaraya Ryokan in Kyoto.

Toray Industries, Inc., established 1926, Tokyo
Toray has expanded its base of synthetic fibers and textiles to include many other fields such as plastics and chemicals, advance composite materials, pharmaceutical and medical products, construction materials, housing, and engineering.

Michiko Uehara, born 1949, Okinawa
Uehara began weaving in 1971 under the direction of Yoshihiro Yanagi in Tokyo and returned to Okinawa three years later where she learned traditional techniques from Shizuko Oshiro. Since opening her studio in 1979 she has participated in numerous exhibitions in Japan.

Urase Co., Ltd., established 1918, Fukui
This company, primarily manufactures polyester fabric with fashion, sports, medical, and industrial applications. Their research and development department, headed by Shigemi Matsuyama, is experimenting with new techniques and technologies for polyester.

Masaji Yamazaki, born 1936, Fukui
Yamazaki is president of Yamazaki Vellodo Co. that specializes in the manufacturing of velvet. He has worked with many notable fashion designers and won numerous Japanese textile awards.

Koichi Yoshimura, born 1939, Fukui
Education: Kobe University
He started working for S. Yoshimura Co., Ltd., in 1966 and has collaborated with many fashion designers including Issey Miyake and Yohji Yamamoto. Recently, he participated in the Tokyo Fashion Fair and in several textile exhibitions in Japan and India.